The|**Ultimate**|Urban Makeover

Unique Architectural Renovations

The | **Ultimate** | Urban **Makeover**

Unique Architectural Renovations

Stephen Crafti

images Publishing

Published in Australia in 2007 by
The Images Publishing Group Pty Ltd
ABN 89 059 734 431
6 Bastow Place, Mulgrave, Victoria 3170, Australia
Tel: +61 3 9561 5544 Fax: +61 3 9561 4860
books@imagespublishing.com
www.imagespublishing.com

National Library of Australia Cataloguing-in-Publication entry:

Crafti, Stephen, 1959– .
The ultimate urban makeover : unique architectural renovations.

Includes index.
ISBN 9781864701715.

1. Architecture, Domestic. 2. Buildings – Repair and reconstruction.
3. Buildings – Additions – Design and construction.
4. Decoration and ornament, Architectural.
5. Architecture, Domestic – Designs and plans. I. Title.

728

ISBN 978 1 86470 171 5

Coordinating editor: Andrea Boekel

Designed by The Graphic Image Studio Pty Ltd, Mulgrave, Australia
www.tgis.com.au
Digital production by Splitting Image Colour Studio Pty Ltd, Australia

Printed by Everbest Printing Co. Ltd., in Hong Kong/China

IMAGES has included on its website a page for special notices in relation to this
and our other publications. Please visit www.imagespublishing.com.

Contents

Introduction

By Stephen Crafti

Renovating a house can be a difficult process even when you're not living in it during construction. And whether you're building a new kitchen or something significantly larger, time is scarce for even the most reliable tradespeople. Add on a couple of months and the budget blows. As those who have renovated will tell you, the process is like a journey. The end may be in sight, but don't start unpacking the furniture and objects just yet.

This book looks at some of the innovative ways in which architects have renovated houses, whether terrace-style homes close to the city or freestanding homes in the suburbs. These projects do not fit into one typology: the diverse mix ranges from homes in Arizona, originally built in the 1940s, to Victorian terrace-style homes in Melbourne; from brownstones in New York to Georgian townhouses in London. The locations are as varied as the building types, but the renovations share the unmistakable hallmarks of architectural design.

How does the old work with the new to create an environment that respects the past but is still relevant today? This is the question faced by the designers whose work is featured in this book. Many of these homes have long and narrow floor plates that bear no relationship to the garden; many have suffered from being spread across several levels. These fundamental problems are addressed with flair and invention by architects who have succeeded in creating integrated environments that flow both inside and out.

Many of the houses featured in this book were built in the 19th or 20th century. The focal point in these homes was the fireplace in the formal sitting room. In addition, gardens in these homes were usually designed for utilitarian purposes, for either accessing the outdoor laundry or toilet. And given the Victorian period's disposition for protection against the natural sunlight, rear façades were often closed to the outdoors. In contrast, the emphasis today is on open-plan living areas adjacent to a garden or courtyard space. The featured projects demonstrate this change in focus and show how the garden has become a feature of the living space.

Other projects demonstrate the skill required to uncover the original bones of a structure that is hidden under well-meaning but unskilled attempts over the years to 'rescue', modernise or enlarge an old house. Lean-tos have often been added to the original home and bathrooms and laundries and kitchens have been awkwardly tacked on. To create a new form for contemporary living is a challenge for today's architects.

Also highlighted are some of the issues relevant to renovating a home. While specific design solutions are tailor-made for each project, common themes are addressed. What materials are the most suitable? What are the best ways of maximising the level of natural light into these homes as well as increasing the ventilation? What were the challenges that had to be overcome? And what advice could the architects and owners pass on to others contemplating a renovation?

As one architect says, "the most successful renovations seem to be those that have retained the essential character of the original home – not only the decorative features such as the fireplaces and cornices, but more importantly, the big architecture of the house such as form, structure, layout, construction and the materials that contribute far more to the personality of any building" (architect Derek Wylie).

A sense of the past is still evident in most of these homes, particularly when they are viewed from the street. But past the front door, new interiors have been carefully interwoven with the past to create striking new homes.

Stephen Crafti

Urban makeovers

The Ultimate Urban Makeover

1950s|classic

New York, New York, USA
Alexander Gorlin Architect LLC

COLOUR

One of the home's distinguishing features is its red façade. Colour also appears in the form of bathroom tiles, such as in the second-floor bathroom featuring rich cobalt tiles. Colour also appears in the confetti-coloured rug in the main living room and in the iconic bright red 1950's furniture designed by Arne Jacobsen.

LIGHT/VENTILATION

Light enters through generous floor-to-ceiling glass windows on the home's façade. Extensive use is made of translucent polycarbonate on the landings and for some of the cabinetry. "There's also cross-ventilation through the home's operable windows, both in the rear and front."

FURNITURE

The house features an impressive array of 1950's classics including an Arne Jacobsen Egg chair in the formal living room. These classics are mixed with iconic pieces from the present such as Philippe Starck lampshades.

ADVICE

In planning your townhouse, make a program or list of rooms and spaces that you need, with approximate square footages. This 'wish-list' will force you to think about how you live now and how you wish to live in the future.

This home, originally designed by J. Paul Mitarachi in 1957 is only a 15-minute train ride from the centre of Manhattan. Bordered by 1930's apartment blocks either side, this classic residence provides a contrast in styles. Featuring floor-to-ceiling windows and spread over three levels, the home is also set back from the street. "The home was originally two-storey. But we were able to extend the house vertically, in line with neighbouring properties," says architect Alexander Gorlin. "The existing two storeys had fallen into disrepair," he adds. ■ The home's interior was entirely gutted, with the exception of some of the finishes on the main floor, including a stair that was reconstructed and brought up to a new third level. "We wanted to respect the vocabulary of the original façade. One of the main changes was using steel structural members rather than the original wooden frame and steel members," says Gorlin, recalling the state of the worn timber. ■ The addition includes a bedroom, study, media room and roof terrace. The media room, which is lined with pear wood cabinets, is acoustically isolated from the rest of the house and is framed with a terrace on one side and an atrium on the other. A large skylight that floods the stair atrium allows light down to the main level through a glass block floor that appears translucent. ■ While the original materials in the house were advanced for their time, they have been refined in a more sophisticated palette. The cabinets in bathrooms and kitchens are finished in baked polyester to reflect the light. The customised laminated glass used for the front panels of the kitchen cabinetry also lightens the interior spaces. "We retained and restored the original travertine floors on the ground floor. But the pear wood, used for the new cabinetry, captures a sense of the 1950s," says Gorlin. ■ The new glass façade of the house announces its presence on the street. In contrast to the open and transparent design is a Zen-inspired stone and moss garden, which provides a contemplative vestibule or air lock, allowing a transition from the hectic city life to the peaceful home within. ■

1 *Façade, set back 25 feet from the footpath, as seen from the street*
2 *Original façade from street, circa 1955*

3 *View from kitchen towards living room and street, circa 1955*

4 *View through entrance vestibule into living room, circa 1955*

5 *Living area, fireplace and stair viewed from dining table*

The Ultimate Urban Makeover

1950s classic

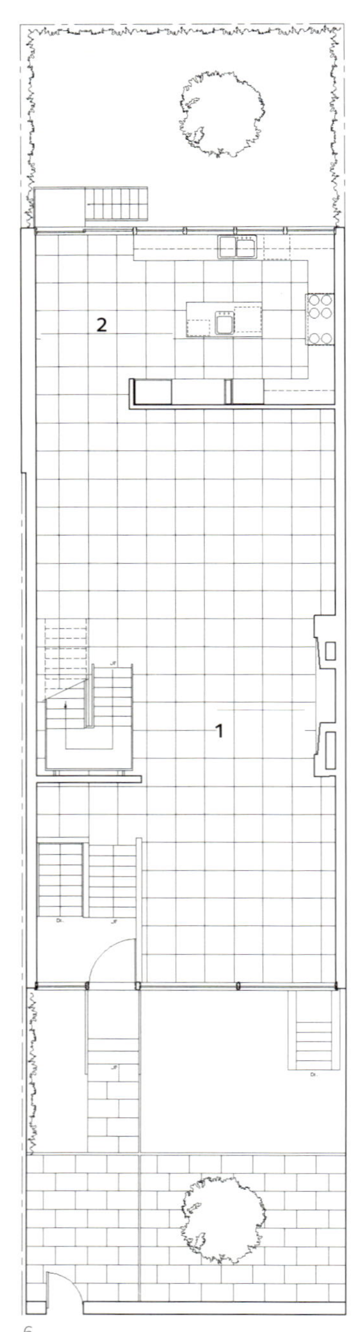

6

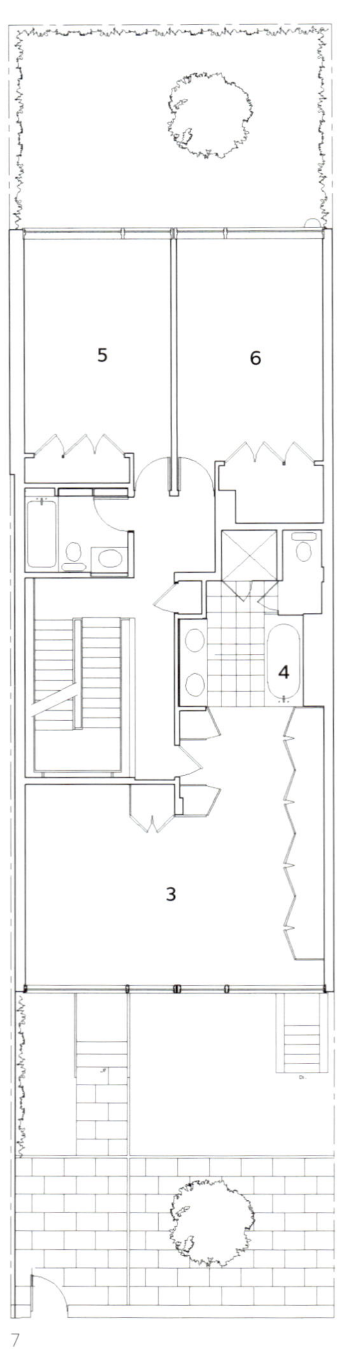

7

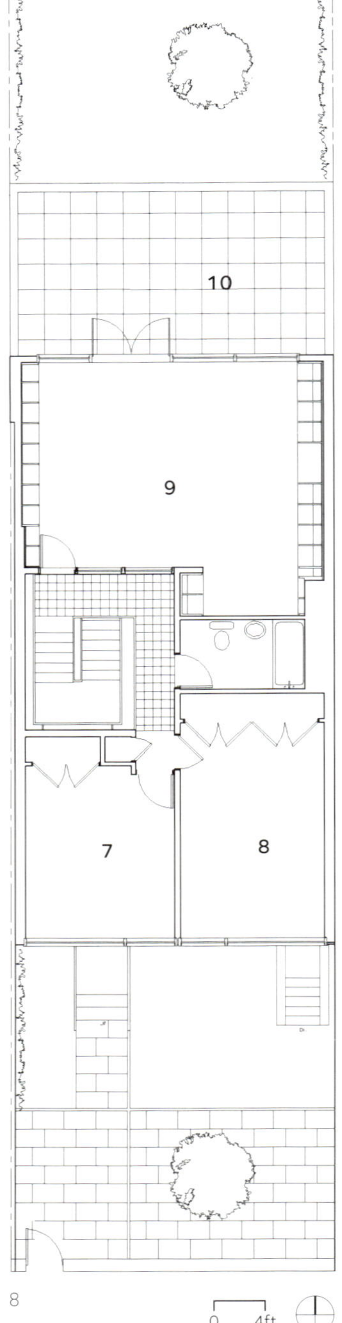

8

0 4ft

1 Living room
2 Kitchen
3 Master bedroom
4 Master bathroom
5 Bedroom 3
6 Bedroom 2
7 Bedroom 4
8 Study
9 Media room
10 Roof terrace

The Ultimate Urban Makeover

1950s classic

10

11

10 Kitchen features stainless steel countertops and LUMAsite translucent polyester cupboards

11 Soundproof media room (viewed from second floor terrace) houses audio equipment and the owner's collection of rare music

12,13 Master bedroom at window wall

14 View into second-floor bathroom from landing

Photography by Peter Aaron/Esto

13

14

12

1

2

The Ultimate Urban Makeover

Basking|in|daylight

Los Angeles, California, USA
Abramson Teiger Architects

COLOUR
A natural palette of materials was chosen, to complement the new light-filled family home. The colours enhance the wood, metal and cement stucco.

MATERIALS
Predominant materials are redwood siding, galvanised sheet metal, cement stucco with natural cement integral color and mill-finish aluminium windows.

LIGHT/VENTILATION
Large walls of windows and a central skylight flood the house with natural light. Strategically placed operable windows and large sliding doors promote cross-ventilation.

ADVICE
It's not always necessary to demolish an existing structure. In this project, the remodel is so comprehensive that there is no sign of the house's previous incarnation. The 'bones' of the original structure were manipulated to form the basis of the transformed house.

The client brief for this suburban renovation was to transform a nondescript, existing house with a maze of rooms into a functional, open-plan family home. ■ Outdoor living and the relationship of the interior to the garden drove the organisation of the very narrow site. The floor plan was manipulated to create a logical flow through the house and to provide glimpse views of the rear garden and pool from the front entry. ■ The architects added to the existing low-ceilinged living room to create two new rooms: the living room and the dining room. The existing ceiling height had to stay, so the horizontal axis was emphasised to play up the low ceiling. ■ On the south side of the house, a maze of small rooms was demolished and a one-and-a-half-storey family room was built. The ceiling height of this room was purposely modulated to offer a different experience from the low horizontal living/dining room. A tall glass wall with large sliding doors opens up completely to the garden and pool. The kitchen opens up to the family room and also has views to the garden and pool. ■ The central hall, connecting the entry to the rear, is punctured with a two-storey towering space capped with a skylight. This space was cut into the highest point of the existing pyramid-shaped roof in a deliberate gesture to open up the middle of the house. The walls in this space literally curve up and outwards through the skylight. The space opens to the sky, flooding the heart of the house with light, and connecting the house visually through its two storeys. ■ The ceilings of the new rooms on the second storey are sculpted and flare up and away from the existing pyramid roof. The curved master bedroom ceiling opens up towards the view. Large sliding windows face the pool and view, while a small square window on the south wall frames a dash of sky from the bed. The second floor is light and airy. ■ The street façade of the house is a quiet collage of form and material that hints at the interior without giving away the secret of the dramatic space within. ■

1   *Street façade before the transformation*
2   *New subtly layered façade*

3

4

5

6

3 *Dramatic two-storey volume opens up towards a skylight that floods the central portion of the house with light*

4 *A large window in the upstairs hallway opens up to a view*

5 *A children's bedroom uses a bright green accent to make the small room feel larger*

6 *View from the breakfast table towards the kitchen and front hall with skylight above*

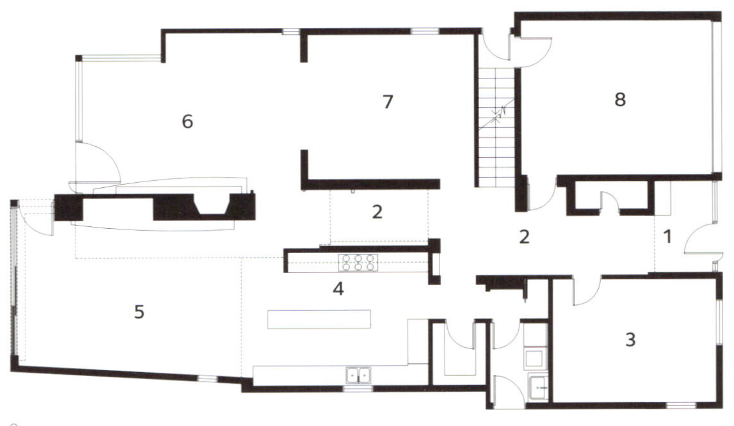

7

8

9

1 Entry
2 Hall
3 Study
4 Kitchen
5 Family room
6 Living room
7 Dining room
8 Garage
9 Open to below
10 Bedroom
11 Bathroom
12 Closet
13 Master bedroom
14 Master bathroom

9

7 Light-filled family room with sliding doors that open to maximise interaction with the garden and swimming pool

8 The low ceiling and horizontal butt glazed window of the living room offer a panoramic view towards the swimming pool

9 Ground floor plan (below); first floor plan (above)

10 Before the renovation, the façade of the house bore no relation to the garden beyond

11 The new garden façade as seen from the swimming pool

Photography by David Lena (2–8,11)
courtesy Abramson Teiger Architects (1,10)

The Ultimate Urban Makeover

1   *View from street prior to renovation*
2   *View from pool across rear courtyard to extension and outdoor dining space*
3   *Street elevation*
4   *View from kitchen through dining space and stair to rear courtyard*
5   *Rear courtyard at dusk*

A|brand|new|slate

Auckland, New Zealand
Crosson Clarke Carnachan Architects

COLOUR

White predominates throughout the house. Silver also appears in the form of aluminium louvres. Colour can be added with a flick of a switch: halogen lights with coloured filters stud the floor and ceiling along the length of the space, allowing the interior space to be 'painted.'

LIGHT/VENTILATION

Light filters into the house by means of skylights, in what was once the original cottage and in the new wing. A glass walkway adjacent to the main bedroom also allows light to penetrate to the kitchen and dining area on the lower level. Light and ventilation is also controlled by external aluminium louvres. Glass sliding doors on the perimeter of the main bedroom allow the breeze to circulate from the ground floor to the upper level.

FURNITURE

The furniture in the house doesn't detract from the home's clean simple lines. Arne Jacobsen plywood chairs in the dining area provide some of the few curves in a largely linear design, as does a circular stainless steel coffee table in the living area. "The furniture (apart from the coffee table) is off the floor rather than anchored to it. We wanted to increase the sense of space," says Simon Carnachan.

ADVICE

Careful planning and sensitivity to the existing architecture is critical for a renovation project like this. Even if initially unforeseen as part of the overall programme, the additional investment in research and preparation will produce a richer result.

From the street, this contemporary home looks like a simple cottage. Built in 1872 as a sea captain's cottage, it is surrounded by modest heritage homes. The owners, architect Simon Carnachan and his wife, interior designer Robyn Carnachan, have transformed it into a superb modern home that shows few signs of the past. ■ The original timber cottage was completely gutted. The only remnants of the original structure are the timber walls and corrugated steel roof. Past the front door, the design is clearly for the 21st century. There are no cornices or skirting boards. There is still a central corridor leading to the two bedrooms, but even it has been partially demolished. ■ A two-storey wing is now attached to the original street-level cottage. Made of concrete, steel and glass, the new wing is concealed behind the original home's pitched roof. "We demolished all the lean-tos and excavated at the back of the house, which falls away from the street. We also removed earth from under the cottage," says Simon Carnachan. The floor area of the house was extended from 80 square metres to 140 square metres. ■ Within the confines of the original cottage are two bedrooms (including the main) and a bathroom, together with two single garages, one on each side of the house. A glass walkway/skylight frames the first level, separating the old from the new and allowing light to penetrate. "The skylight (above the main bedroom suite) and glass bridge create a link between the original and new," says Carnachan. The new kitchen, dining and living area can be viewed from the first level and are accessed by a steel and glass staircase. Sandblasted sliding glass walls on the edge of the main bedroom create privacy from the living areas below. External aluminium louvres on the new wing create privacy from neighbours and diffuse the natural sunlight. ■ While the house appears as a white canvas, colour can be added from halogen lights that are placed in the walls and ceilings. "Coloured filters in the halogen lights give us the opportunity of splashing out with colour without bringing in different furniture and artwork," says Robyn Carnachan. The materials selected for the project were restricted to glass, stone, stainless steel and New Zealand tawa timber flooring. "It's a small space, so the design was about using fewer, rather than more finishes and materials," she adds. ■

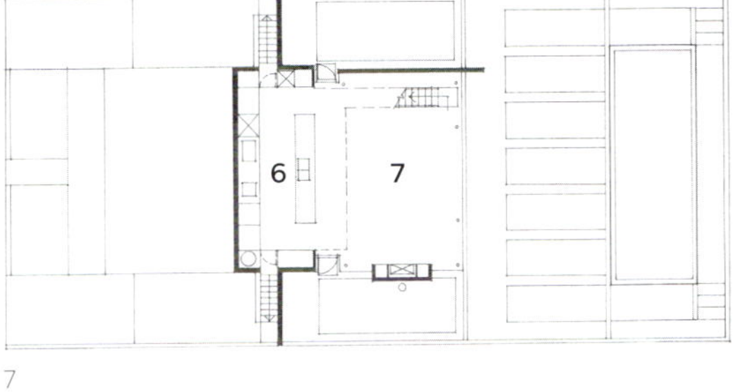

6

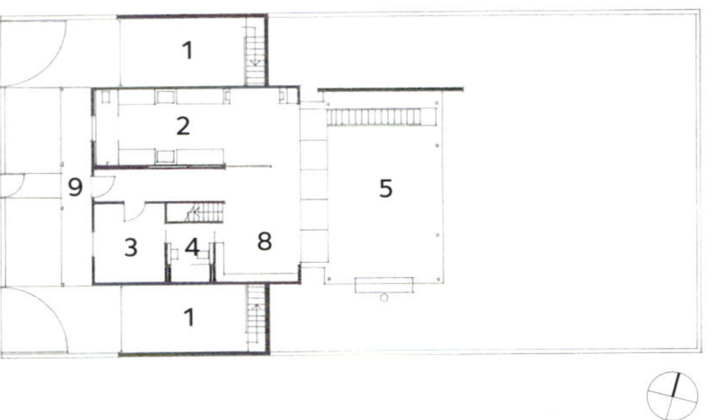

8

9

7

1 Garage
2 Main bedroom/bathroom combined
3 Bedroom
4 Bathroom
5 Void
6 Kitchen
7 Dining/Living
8 Library
9 Verandah

11

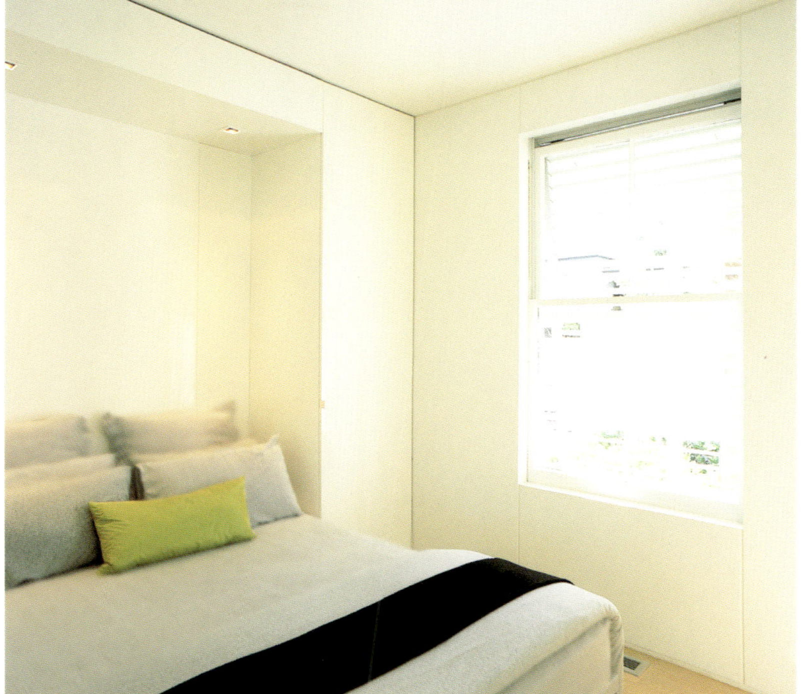

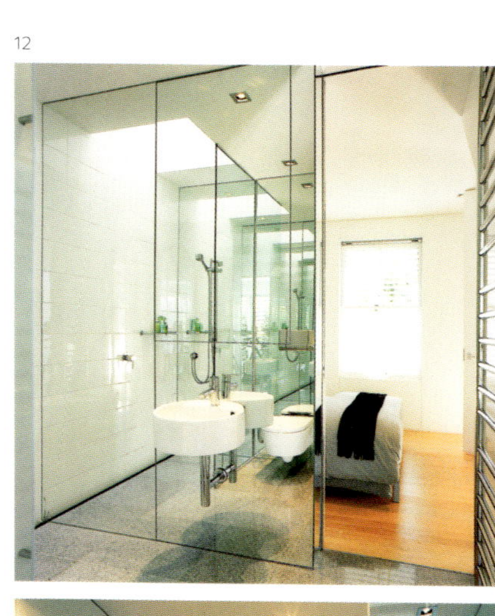

6 *Living and dining space opening to grassed rear courtyard and pool*

7 *Ground floor plan (above); first floor plan (below)*

8,10 *Kitchen and dining space with glazed link over*

9 *Kitchen*

11 *Guest bedroom*

12 *Guest bedroom ensuite*

13 *Main bedroom ensuite*

Photography by Patrick Reynolds

12

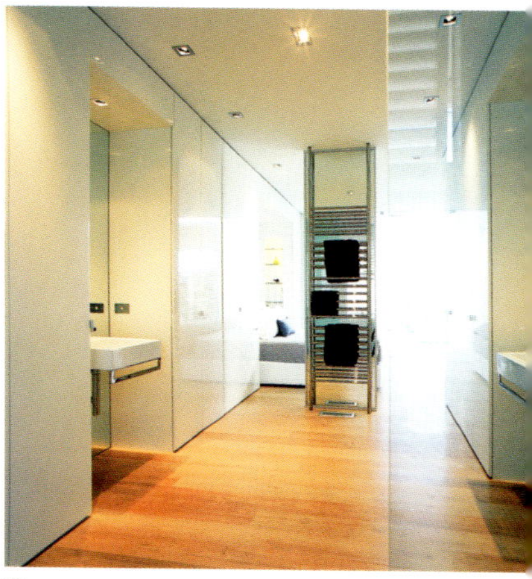

13

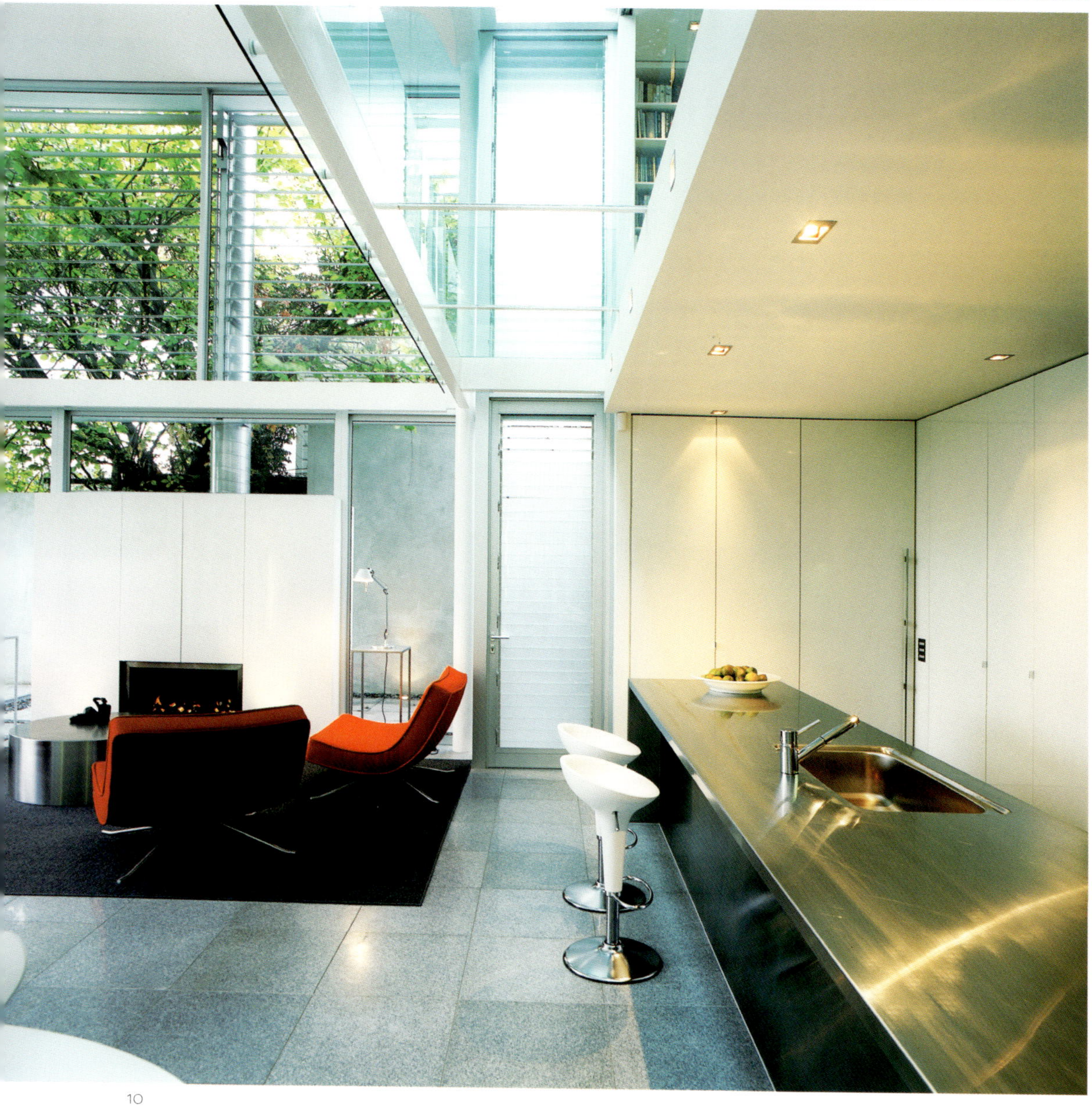

10

1

Breaking|away

London, UK

Henning Stummel Architects Ltd

Colour

The exterior colour scheme was influenced by the shades of colour in the London stock brick. The external planks were pre-painted in different shades to allow for manoeuvrability on site. Internally, the walls are painted white; the MDF joinery has a lacquer finish.

The perspex fenestration strips are part of the external skin. A camouflage idea was developed, using five different shades of grey, to take advantage of the grey appearance of the perspex during the day

Light

The perspex strips in the new addition allow diffused light to enter into the new bathrooms. The bathrooms feature sliding doors, allowing light to filter into the original rear rooms of the townhouse.

Ventilation

The existing structure of the house was not altered. But with the creation of the new wing, the size of some of the rooms, such as the bedroom on the top floor was increased.

Furniture

The house is filled with mainly contemporary furniture, with a sprinkling of classic pieces.

Advice

"I suppose you have to anticipate that everything ends up taking longer than you expect. For people seeking instant gratification, it would not be ideal to renovate a Georgian townhouse like this one. The first major complexity was getting planning permission. That took an amazing 18 months and was only achieved on appeal. And unlike our experience, try not to live on site."
– Henning Stummel

There's no question as to what is original and what has been added to this Georgian townhouse in London. The striated timber addition clearly stands apart from the multi-storey brick home. "There is an aesthetic of tall rectangular portrait formats throughout Georgian architecture: the elevations, the window formats and the subdivision of the windows," says architect Henning Stummel, who created the same proportions with this addition to his own home. ■ Built in the boom after the Napoleonic wars, between 1820 and 1830, the heritage-listed house is the smallest type of London four-storey townhouse with two rooms on each floor. "Originally each room would have been let out individually. It's hard to believe, but some rooms would have accommodated entire families," he says. "Because it was built for the poor, there was no special craftsmanship," adds Stummel, who likens the original construction to 'drunken sailors holding each other up.' ■ All the original rooms of the townhouse were retained. To the approximately 100 square metres of floor space, Stummel added 15 square metres with the new rectangular addition. The main problem with the townhouse was that it only had one bathroom at the top level and it took up an entire room. By creating the extension, the bathroom became part of the new wing, freeing up the entire top floor for his daughter's bedroom. The extension now accommodates two bathrooms and a utility space. ■ One of the reasons shiplapped boards were used for the new wing (apart from making a clear distinction between past and present), was due to access to the property. "All the materials had to be brought through the house. The extension was assembled within the small garden. Timber construction allowed us to minimise the wet trades and make use of a compact type of construction," says Stummel. The new wing projects onto a disused chimneystack; the fireplaces had been removed a many years ago. ■ The bathrooms and storage area in the addition have been lined from floor to ceiling in white transparent perspex, which has the same dimensions as the timber boards. "The timber relates to the original home. A large part of the Georgian house was built in pine wood," says Stummel, referring to the varnished pine floors throughout the house. ■

1 The extension is a deliberate contrast to the existing townhouse

2

2 *Early evening view of
extension*

3 *Ground-floor utility room*

4 *View from kitchen into
utility room*

Photography by Luke Caulfield

The Ultimate Urban Makeover

4

3

1

2

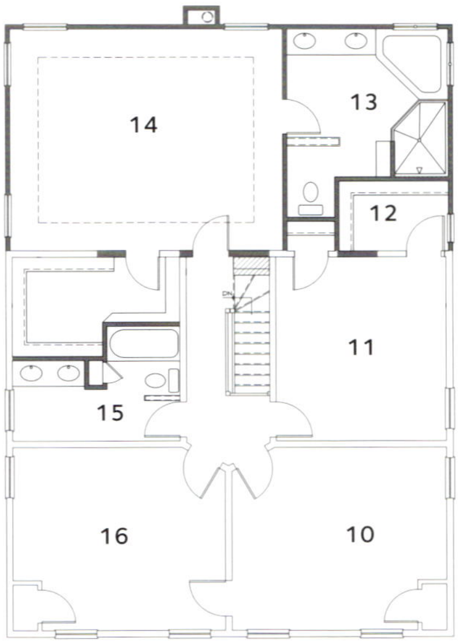

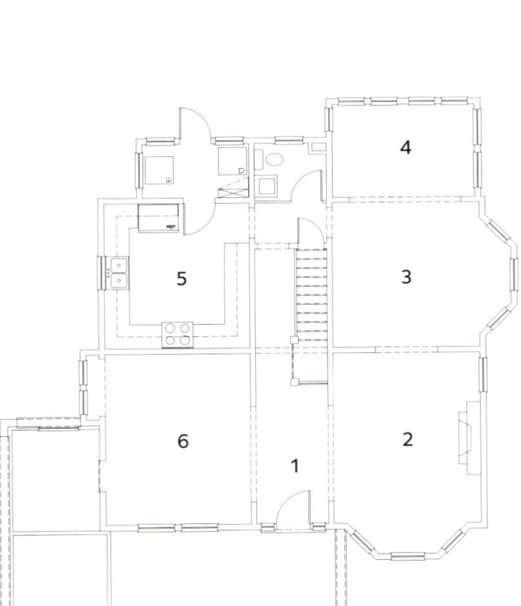

1 Foyer
2 Living room
3 Dining room
4 Sunroom
5 Kitchen
6 Sitting room
7 Bedroom
8 Bedroom
9 Sitting room
10 Bedroom
11 Bedroom

1 Existing covered porch
2 Existing foyer
3 Office
4 Existing dining room
5 Powder room
6 Utility/mudroom/laundry
7 Family room
8 Kitchen
9 Existing sitting room
10 Existing bedroom
11 Existing bedroom
12 WC
13 Master bathroom
14 Master bedroom
15 Hall bathroom
16 Existing bedroom

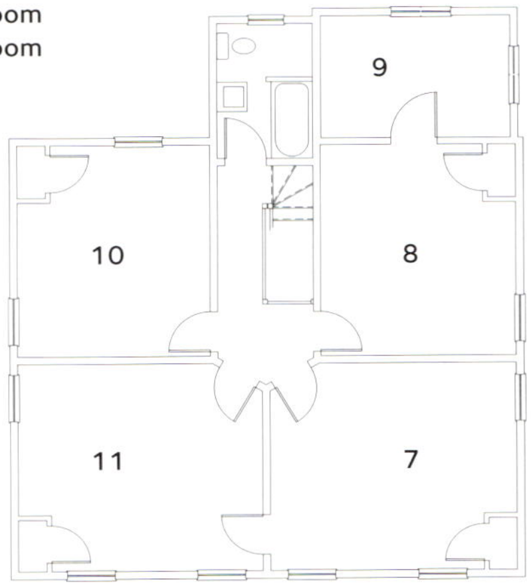

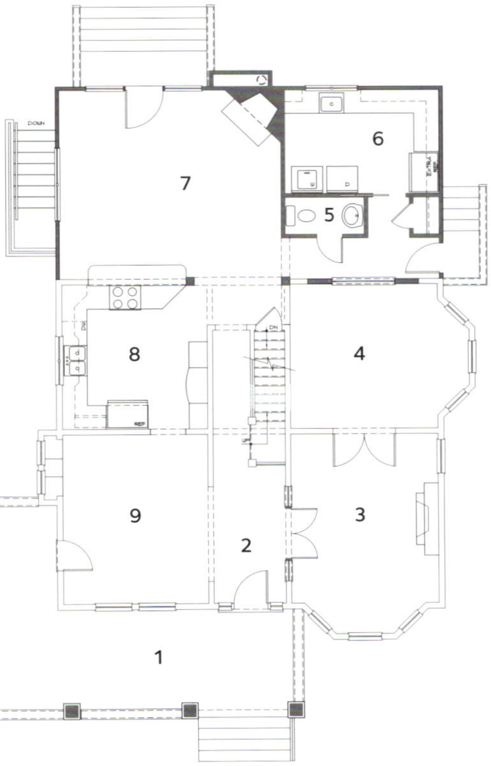

3

4

5

6

The Ultimate Urban Makeover

Bungalow|makeover

Catonsville, Maryland, USA
Architecture by Design

LIGHT/VENTILATION

Over the years, the several poorly planned additions to the house had compromised the original design. Removing the porch addition and applied shutters and installing new windows around the house dramatically increased light and ventilation.

COLOUR

The original exterior colour palette was dark and dank. The dark paint was removed and appropriate trim around doors and windows was added. The owner chose a light taupe colour opaque stain along with a bright white trim and bracket colour. These updated colours allowed the detail of the rough sawn shakes as well as the curves of the brackets to shine through. Inside, the existing spaces had many layers of paint and wallpaper that were stripped down to the original plaster walls. These areas were painted with a light colour to reflect the natural light and contrast the inlaid wood floors. Light cabinetry and black granite counters in the kitchen provide a modern yet still nostalgic feel to the space.

ADVICE

When confronted with an outdated historic home that lacks the modern amenities and open spaces of a newer home, addressing the 'bones' of a structure is key. Consider what you may salvage out of the original structure along with what you would like to see improved. Is the amount of original charm that drew you to the place still intact or has the potential renovation rendered the original charm undiscernible? In this case a full-width addition to the rear extended the original massing so that the new seamlessly blended with the old. Modern technologies allow long spans and wider open spaces also achieving the feel of a newer design within the parameters of a historic skin.

Built in 1915, this two-storey bungalow- or craftsman-style home had a full front porch, cedar shake siding and accent brackets on the gables. ■ Unfortunately, the siding was deteriorating, decorative shutters had been added, the porch had an unsightly corner addition and the accent brackets at the gables had been covered in aluminium siding. It was in dire need of refurbishment. ■ The prospective owners were keen to evaluate if the house was a candidate for renovation and addition. It was an overwhelming prospect for them to consider this substantial purchase only to find that demolition was the only choice. The verdict from the architect was that the house was suitable to undergo renovations and additions. ■ The rear of the house was extended by 18 feet on all levels, providing the space to expand the kitchen and to add a family room, laundry and powder room on the first floor, with access from the parking area. ■ As part of the remodel, the porch addition was removed and the shake siding was repaired, repainted and enhanced. The applied shutters were removed and a more appropriate trim was added, along with new windows around the entire home. The aluminium siding was removed from the brackets, exposing a detailed curved pattern that was then replicated for the rear extension. ■ Every room underwent a refurbishment: wallpaper was removed, paint stripped and the wood flooring was revealed. The second-floor addition provided the space for the master suite and a separate master bath. The hall bath was previously located at the centre rear of the house and was small and out of date. Since a substantial amount of space was being added to the second floor, it made sense to borrow part of the existing rear bedroom and convert that into a new hall bathroom. ■ This makeover resulted in the home gaining its original sparkle. It has an open, contemporary feel, but maintains the charm and character of a turn-of-the-century home. ■

1   *The existing front façade was dark, unattractive and lacked period detail*
2   *The house has regained its former sparkle*
3   *Floor plans before*
4   *Floor plans after*
5   *The existing kitchen was cramped and disconnected from other spaces*
6   *The new kitchen is open to the new family room addition and provides an abundance of light into these spaces*
7   *A small corner of an existing bedroom now houses the new hall bathroom*
8   *The rear corner of the new addition is the optimal place for an enlarged master bathroom with corner soaking tub and walk-in shower*

7

8

Photography by Judith A. Miller
Charles Pruett

1

2

3

Carefully|folded

London, UK

Alison Brooks Architects

COLOUR

All the internal walls are painted white. The few colours that do appear in the interior are generated from natural finishes such as the timber floors.

LIGHT/VENTILATION

A large glazed strip, approximately 9 metres by 1.5 metres, separates the existing house and the new extension. All ventilation was passively designed, with large sliding doors leading to the new deck. A bespoke trickle vent runs along the length of the new roof light.

ADVICE

Sometimes it's best to employ a young practice. A recently formed practice will put the time and effort in that is required. An older, more established practice would not necessarily give you the level of commitment required to execute what are often barely profitable jobs.

1,2 *Roof geometry creates a new 'landscape' when seen from upper-storey windows*

3 *View from garden*

Located in leafy Cheswick, this house is surrounded by Victorian housing. The picturesque area also features several late Edwardian semi-detached and detached houses. "Escalating house prices have meant gap sites are being in-filled. Many private house owners are also reinvesting in their properties with basement and rear extensions," says architect Alison Brooks. ■ The Edwardian house was built in 1890 by a private developer who was responsible for constructing the entire street. "It's understandable that he retained this house for himself. It has the largest garden in the neighbourhood," says Brooks. The architects were not only fortunate to work with a large site – they were also asked to extend a house that was in good condition, with many period features still intact.

■ The brief was to provide additional open-plan living space opening onto the garden. "The clients wanted the space to perform a number of different functions for their busy family," says Brooks. "They also wanted to be able to look out from their bedroom onto a beautiful roof," she adds. ■ The new extension makes a bold contrast with the existing house. By using a single material for the entire extension, its form and geometry were manipulated without creating something that was fighting with the architecture of the original house. The angular planes of the new extension relate to the many angled gables of the existing Edwardian roof. ■ The subtle tonal similarity between the London stock brick from which the existing house is constructed, and the Brazilian hardwood cladding of the new extension, ties the whole composition together. Internally, the timber floor continues from the terrace through the new extension into the kitchen. To accentuate the form of the extension, the finishes used in the kitchen are pared back, and include lacquered MDF cupboards.

■ While the extension is one large space, it affords a variety of spatial conditions for the owners. The shifts in the pitch roof for example, create a low and intimate dining area, a lofty living space with views to the garden, and a sheltered portico for covered, but outdoor living. ■ Alison Brooks Architects received a RIBA Award and the Stephen Lawrence Prize for this project in 2006. ■

1 Formal dining
2 Study
3 Living room
4 Kitchen
5 WC
6 Dining
7 Living
8 Deck
9 Covered deck
0 10m

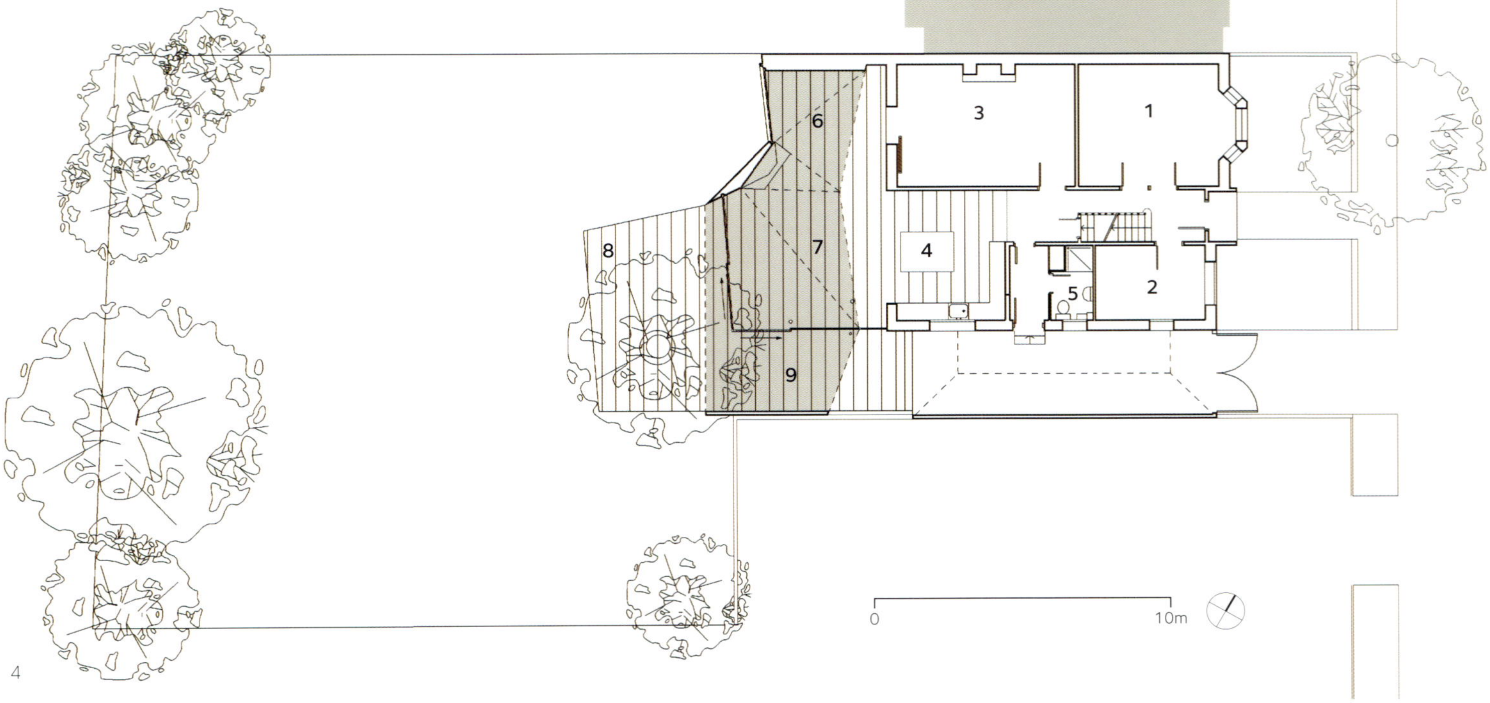

7

4 Floor plan
5 Strip between house and extension
6 The fireplace acts as a transition between lower and higher spaces
7 Column-free corner with sliding windows
8 Kitchen in existing house volume

Photography by Cristobal Palma (3,5–10)
courtesy Alison Brooks Architects (1,2,4)

8

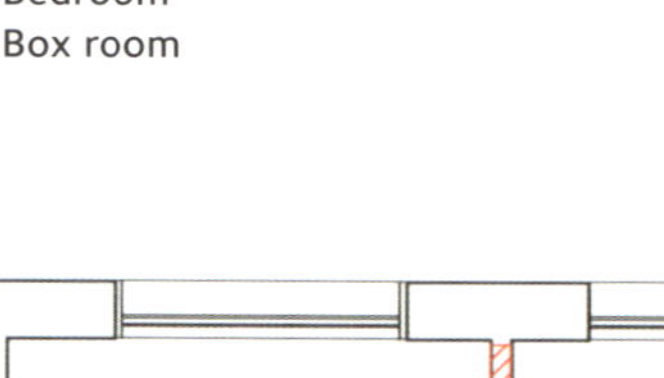

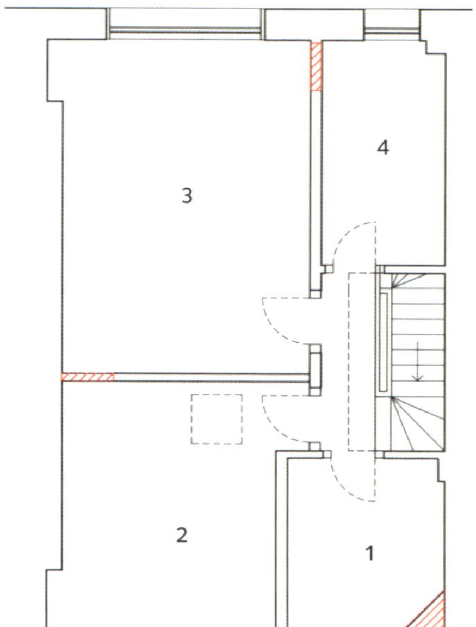

1 Children's bathroom
2 Bedroom
3 Bedroom
4 Box room

1 Children's bathroom
2 Bedroom
3 Stair landing
4 Utility room
5 WC
6 Bedroom

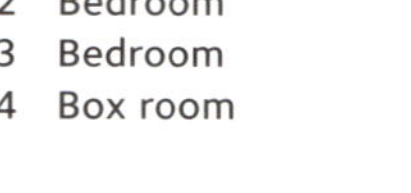

The Ultimate Urban Makeover

Classic | contemporary | approach

Notting Hill, London, UK
Modern Architectural Practice

This property is typical of many terraced Victorian houses in London's Notting Hill area. The renovation plan for this house was to extend it by adding a loft within the roof space. In addition, all the rooms required refurbishment, as they were poorly altered and decorated. The new rooms and decoration provide much-needed space for the family and a unique expression of their lifestyle. As the house was located in a conservation area, no external alterations or additions were proposed. After granting planning permission, the local council imposed a condition that even the new skylights within the roof loft space had to be constructed and recessed so that the existing shape of the roof remained unaltered. ■ The strategy was to retain the original proportions of the house and to add as little as possible. All existing important architectural features such as the cornices, architraves and dado rails were retained and restored. A requirement for a generous amount of storage space was addressed sensitively, without altering the room proportions. The rooms were stripped back to their original proportions and the minimal interventions, in the form of floor-standing dividing screens and new built-in furniture, provide a sense of calm sophistication. Rooms were opened up, allowing spaces to interconnect, reducing the formality of the original Victorian spaces. ■

COLOUR

The east–west orientation of the house, which provides abundant natural light, influenced the selection of the materials and colour palette. A palette of warm greys in materials and paints softens the quality of light into the interiors.

Black walnut timber was chosen for the floors, furniture and floor-standing screens, creating the impression that the screens and furniture have been carved out of the floor. All the bathrooms feature natural grey limestone flooring and low limestone walls that conceal storage troughs. The limestone and etched glass wall panels provide a counterpoint to the black walnut timber flooring.

LIGHT/VENTILATION

All the rooms had good natural light and ventilation, so no additional fenestration was needed on the front and rear elevations. However, skylights were added to provide natural lighting to new roof loft space and central stairwell, previously devoid of natural light. The traditional sash-operated windows were not sealed at the edges, to allow natural trickle ventilation into the rooms.

FURNITURE

Classic swan chairs by Arne Jacobsen and contemporary breakfast stools by Jasper Morrisson accentuate and contrast with the family's collection of antiques. Vintage Edwardian sofas were re-covered to update their appeal in the new environment.

ADVICE

When faced with government conservation planning restrictions or a tight budget, it is important to establish that the basics are correct, for they cannot be changed. A sense of proportion in the volume, variety in types of spaces and good natural light are fundamental elements. A coherent and thoughtful palette of materials, colour and textures is essential.

1   *Restoration of the kitchen opening, in progress*
2   *Restoration of the arch detail opposite the kitchen, in progress*
3   *Second floor plan before*
4   *Second floor plan after*
5   *New galley kitchen*
6   *Restored opening into the kitchen adjoining the dining room*
7   *New streamlined bathroom*
8   *The existing Victorian façade remains untouched*

Photography by Sarah Jones

8

Colorado|modern

Denver, Colorado, USA
Hutton Ford Architects

COLOUR

Color trends and preferences change overtime. "I usually apply timeless color solutions to the more permanent architectural materials and use color on the painted surfaces", says Alan Ford.

When possible, locate windows within a given room with multiple exposures to provide direct sunlight throughout the day. Proportion of windows to the room: 25 percent window area to floor area is a good rule of thumb.

FURNITURE

Niches and operable window seats were created for practical and 'comfort' reasons; built-in bookcases and storage areas were placed at the low ceiling locations on the second floor to allow them to be functional.

ADVICE

When designing addition/renovation projects it is important to do your homework. Approach the project as an archeological investigation, peeling away the layers of the existing architecture to gain a clear understanding of the original aesthetic intent and construction methodology. Once that work is completed the design solution will usually reveal itself.

This project consisted of an 1100-square-foot, two-storey addition to a 1600-square-foot Victorian house built in 1896. The residence is in an urban neighbourhood of eclectic architectural styles, ranging from Victorian residences to suburban bungalows. ■ The program included renovating and expanding the existing kitchen, adding a family room and breakfast area and a second-floor master bedroom, to create a 2700-square-foot home. ■ Underlying organizing principles found in the 1896 architecture are incorporated into the addition: datums expressed as projected brick bands that organize windows and brick arches, masonry details, roof slopes and vertical proportions. Double-hung windows, 45-degree roof pitch, Victorian accent shingles, Colorado red sandstone window sills and brick arches defined by projected soldier rowlocks also match features found in the original house. The openness of a 1970s renovation was also maintained in the addition. ■ The existing kitchen was doubled in size and expanded. An east-facing breakfast area is located at the end of the kitchen, adjacent to an outdoor deck. The kitchen and breakfast area have direct views into the new family room. ■ The floor of the new family room is 16 inches lower than the existing main floor to provide an 11-foot ceiling. Soffits and arches provide rhythm, define space and take the eye to the sandstone fireplace at the south wall. The roof and ceiling also step up at the fireplace to give a sense of visual lift and direct the eye upwards along the tapered lines of the fireplace, terminating in ridge skylights, which wash the sandstone in natural light. ■ Also at the south wall, the exterior Flemish bond brick with its recessed header pattern is continued inside and out to provide color and texture. The structural columns between the family room and the kitchen areas create an arched entry feature and provide rhythm and a visual break at the point where the floor level changes. ■ In the interior, structural elements and varied ceiling planes are used to define space and direct the eye. Low-cost materials add to the simple expression, which is evident at the second-floor bedroom where the roof and structural forms define the character of the space. ■ The gables, dormers and the 45-degree pitch of the addition provided an opportunity to add character to and define space within the master suite. The structural ridge beams and structural columns are expressed – the ceiling fan is located at the cross-point of two ridge beams. Low ceiling areas are made functional with built-in bookshelves and storage; the south dormer provides a natural canopy for the bed. ■

2

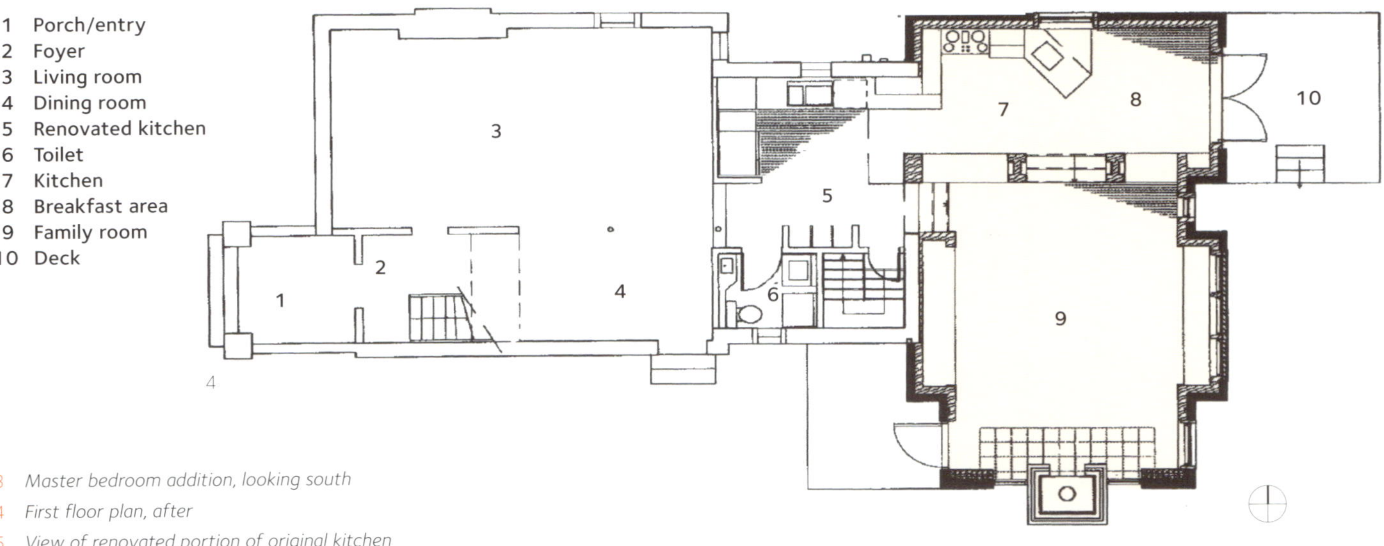

3

1 Porch/entry
2 Foyer
3 Living room
4 Dining room
5 Renovated kitchen
6 Toilet
7 Kitchen
8 Breakfast area
9 Family room
10 Deck

4

3 Master bedroom addition, looking south
4 First floor plan, after
5 View of renovated portion of original kitchen
6 Second floor plan, after

The Ultimate Urban Makeover

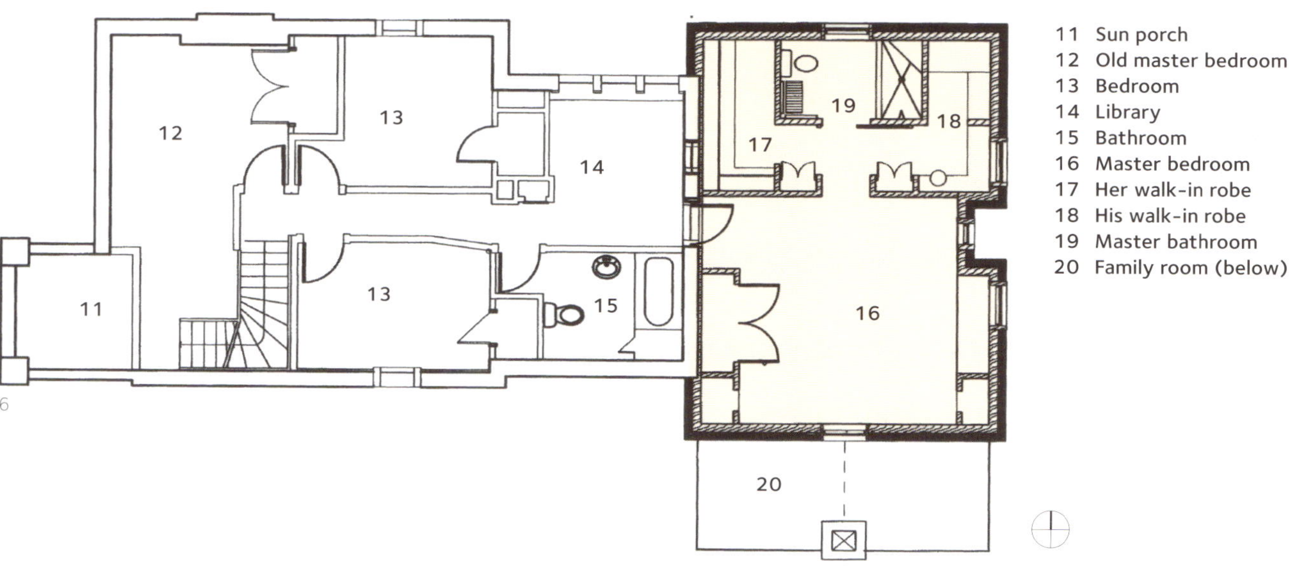

5

6

11 Sun porch
12 Old master bedroom
13 Bedroom
14 Library
15 Bathroom
16 Master bedroom
17 Her walk-in robe
18 His walk-in robe
19 Master bathroom
20 Family room (below)

7

7 Family room addition
8 View from family room addition into the kitchen
9 Master bathroom addition

Photography by Jackie Shumaker (1,2,9)
Ron Johnson (3,5,7,8)

1

2

3

4

The Ultimate Urban Makeover

A|conservation|area

London, UK

Charles Barclay Architects

Colour

Colour appears in the materials. The dark walnut floors in the living areas, for example, contrast with the modulated daylight.

Light

Several elements bring light into the house. A new sculptured skylight was inserted above the staircase. There is also a new skylight over the kitchen. Bi-fold doors leading from the conservatory also increase the light levels significantly. A specially coated glass was used to reduce the harsher sunlight, particularly in the conservatory.

Furniture

The clients chose contemporary furniture that complements built-in furniture, such as the bench seat in the living areas, designed by the architects. They wanted the furniture to reflect the same clean and minimal lines of the architecture.

Advice

It's important to make these houses feel spaciously generous, even though they are quite restrictive. Getting light into these terraces is crucial. Using a good architect will expedite an interesting design through the planning process.

1. Bay window and cantilevered brickwork of new extension
2. New extension in context, with conservatory element and original house beyond
3. Generous glazing of the garden elevation allows winter sunlight to penetrate deep into the house
4. Conservatory and dining areas merge to provide expansive diagonal sight lines

This 1860's townhouse is located in Battersea, in London's southwest. While the house isn't classified, it is in a conservation area, surrounded by many homes of the same period. "It's a typical Victorian suburban street. It's leafy and there's a gentle slope," says architect Charles Barclay, who first saw the house in a derelict state. "It was in extremely poor condition. There was a substandard rear extension that had to be completely demolished," he adds. ■ While the original formal front rooms (living and dining rooms) were retained, the walls between were removed to create a continuous flow of space. The front and middle bedrooms on the first floor were also retained in the renovation. However, a tacked-on conservatory at the rear of the home was demolished. The original kitchen/informal living area was completely redesigned for contemporary living. "The key to the project was to increase the size of the new kitchen and casual living area," says Barclay. "The owners wanted clean lines and spaces that were light. The word quality was also used." The brief also included a new main bedroom and bathroom on the first floor. ■ The architects were inspired by some of the sculptural features of the original home, such as the curved walls in the hall and by the stair. These features were given a contemporary feel by stripping away all of the detail, such as the cornice work. The original staircase was retained, but fussy timber balustrades were replaced by a low wall with the original handrail reinstated. ■ The most striking aspects of the renovation are the new kitchen, informal dining and living areas. A large bay window in the dining area overlooks the rear garden and floor-to-ceiling glass bi-fold doors lead from the conservatory to the garden deck. Although the garden elevation of the new extension is modern and cantilevers over the bay window, the architects used reclaimed London stock brick to create a link with the original home. The original pine floors were removed and replaced with a walnut floor. The materials used in the kitchen, such as concrete benches, are strong and contemporary. "The extension is unashamedly modern. This is a house from the 19th century that has been entirely adapted for living in the 21st century," says Barclay, who cites Mies van der Rohe as one of his influences. ■

5 *Ground floor plan*
6 *First floor plan*
7 *Stair balustrade treatment lends a sculptural quality to the hall*

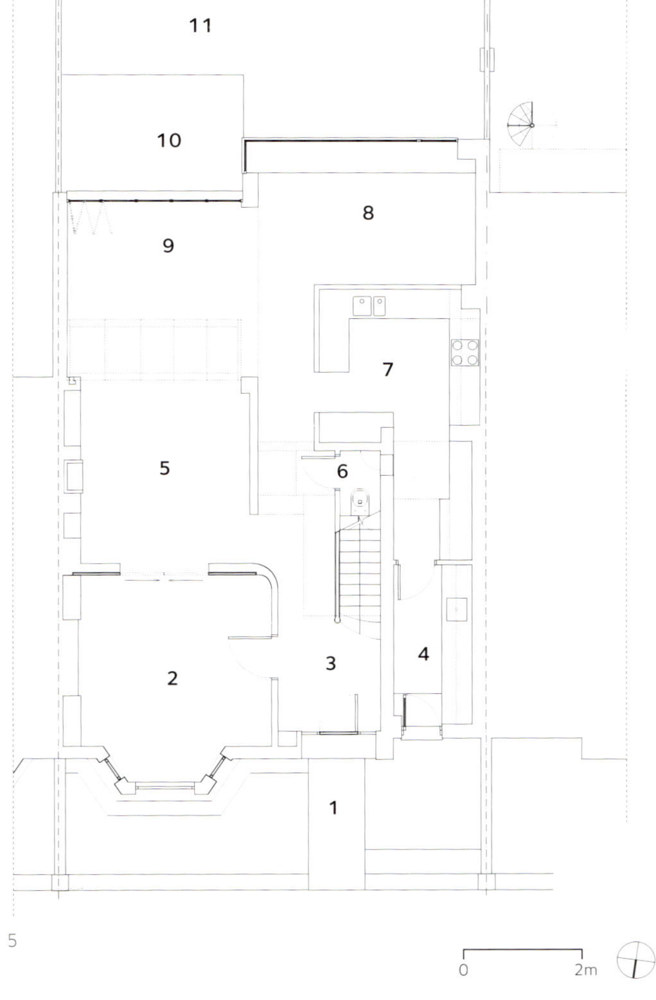

5

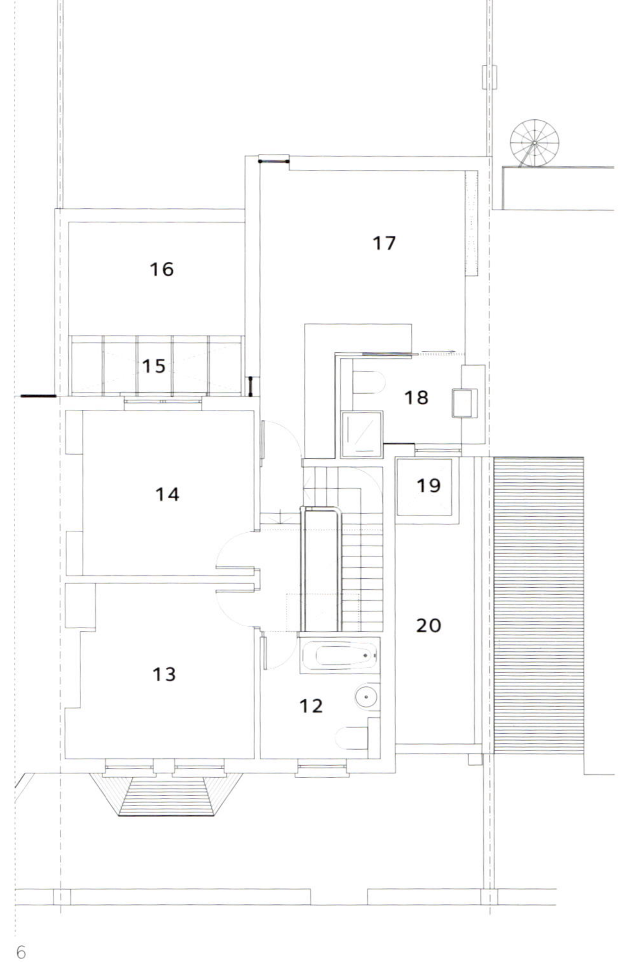

6

1	Entrance	11	Garden
2	Study	12	Bathroom 2
3	Hall	13	Bedroom 3
4	Utility	14	Bedroom 2
5	Living area	15	Rooflight
6	WC	16	Flat roof
7	Kitchen	17	Bedroom 1
8	Dining area	18	Bathroom 1
9	Conservatory area	19	Rooflight
10	Terrace	20	Flat roof

8   *View from dining area towards living spaces across corner
     of kitchen counter*

9   *Star-like geometry of new roof light over stair*

10   *With doors removed, the corridor becomes part of the
     ground floor's flowing space*

11   *Original curved wall leads from living room to hallway*

Photography by David Grandorge (1,4,7,8,11)
Sinisa Savic (2,3,9,10)

9

11

10

1

1 *New addition viewed from back garden showing spatial continuity between indoors and outdoors*

2 *View from first floor prior to construction; this space is now the entry to the addition at this level*

3 *Double-height glazed space between new and existing allows southern daylight to penetrate deep into the space*

4 *Anti-space at new entrance indicates deconstructed corner and vertical louvres that restrict views to interior on approach*

2

3

A|contemporary|box

Dublin, Ireland

Box Architecture

COLOUR

The selection of materials, whether timber or limestone, determined the main colours used within the home. Painted area are white.

LIGHT

To maximise natural light within the home, the architects extended the ground floor into the garden.

FURNITURE

While the owners are currently looking for new furniture, some of it was built-in, designed by Box Architecture.

ADVICE

Make sure you communicate your brief clearly to an architect. Dialogue between client and architect is a crucial part of the design process.

This renovated and extended 1940's house is located on a leafy suburban boulevard in the north of Dublin. Typical of its period, the stucco and brick house was fairly dark before the renovation. ■ The strategy was to design three built forms at the rear of the house, to create six distinct spaces. "The client brief was to provide an additional main bedroom and ensuite bathroom, together with larger kitchen and living spaces on the ground floor," says architect David Dwyer, who, while appreciating the original home, could also see its shortcoming for contemporary living. All the rooms in the existing house, with the exception of the kitchen (renovated in the 1960s), were retained in the new design. "The large north-facing rear garden was the driving force behind the form of the new wing," says Dwyer. ■ The transition between the new and old is immediately apparent on approach to the building. A corner of the original house was removed to allow a timber-wrapped screen to form an 'anti-space' upon arrival. On approach through the front gate, the alteration of the side access becomes apparent by the imitation of the normal garage door arrangement. This produces a spatial enclosure on two edges, with a new entrance screen that deconstructs the corner of the house. Vertical timber louvres are used to prevent views into the home. ■ The extension is composed of three elements juxtaposed in three dimensions. Each element features a different material. On the ground floor is a brick-clad box. On the first floor is a concrete rendered box. The box adjacent to the entrance is clad in timber. Sliding and folding screens, which allow the three spaces to be divided, are placed between these elements. To achieve a sense of fluidity, a limited palette of materials, such as limestone flooring, was used throughout. ■ The two courtyards that flank the family room are significant features of the renovation. Light now penetrates into the new kitchen and meals area that leads from the family room, as well as back into the study at the front of the house. Introducing light into the house was one of the most crucial aspects of the design. "We could have increased the amount of space at ground level by using the courtyard spaces. But we felt it was more important to create quality light-filled spaces that our clients would enjoy," says Dwyer. ■

5   *The existing front living room was retained*
6   *New spaces viewed on entry allow glimpses to rear garden*
7   *View of daylight in kitchen, courtyard and rear garden; screen wall is half-open*
8   *First floor plan*
9   *Ground floor plan*
10   *Night view from rear garden with all internal screens open*

Photography by Paul Tierney

5

6

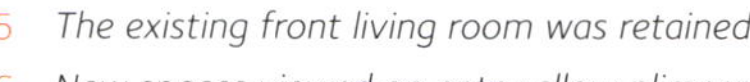

7

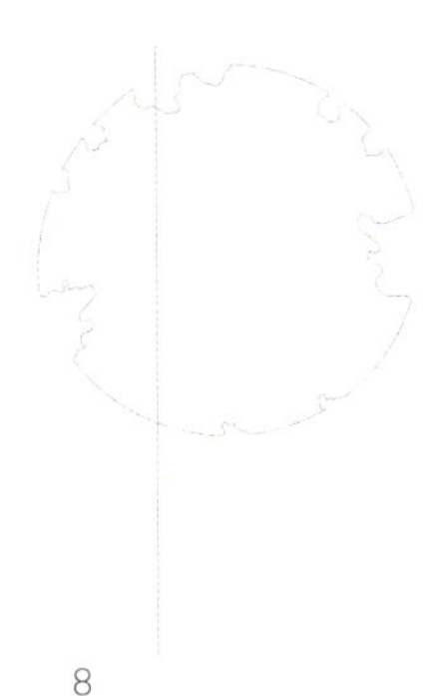

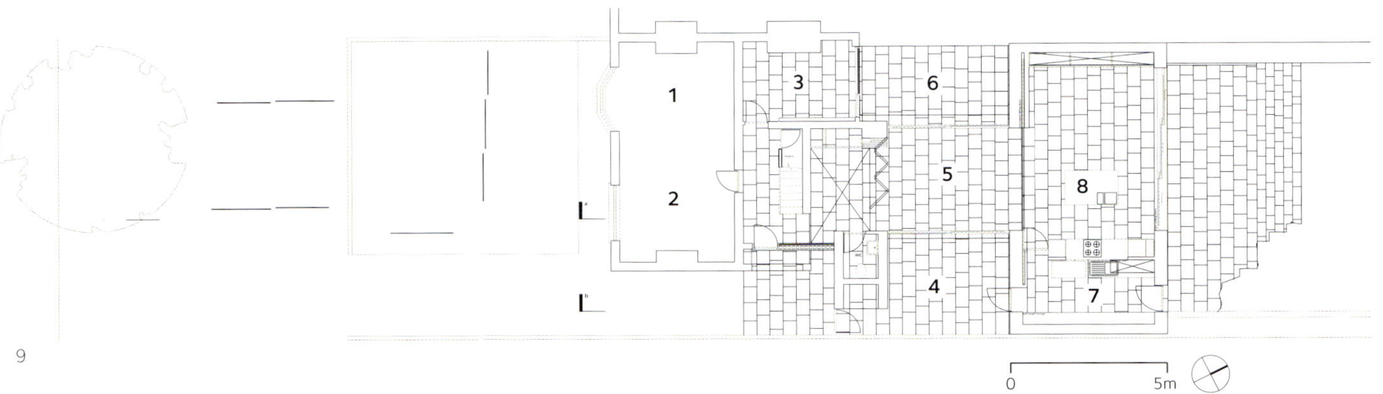

8

9

1 Living
2 Dining
3 Study
4 Courtyard
5 Family room
6 Courtyard
7 Utility room
8 Kitchen
9 Bedroom 1
10 Bedroom 2
11 Bedroom 3
12 Bathroom
13 Ensuite
14 Master bedroom

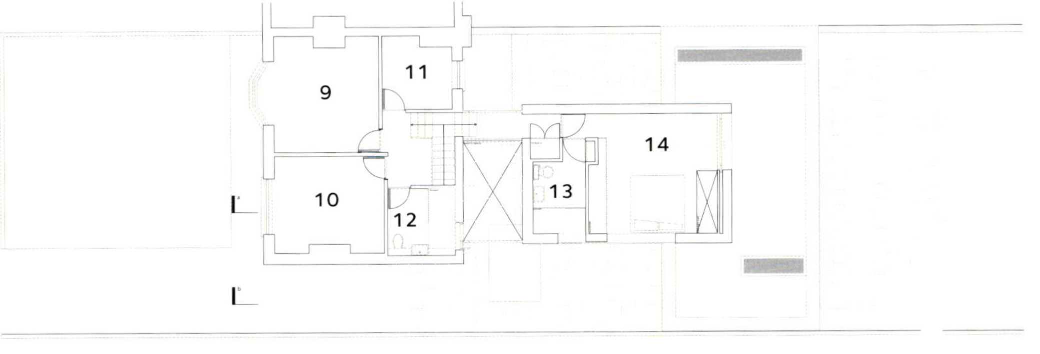

10

Creating|two|zones

Carlton, Victoria, Australia

Suzanne Dance, Architect

COLOUR

The only colour used in the renovation appears in the painted timber windows framing the main bedroom. "The steel can feel quite cold. The red adds a sense of warmth. But my clients are quite extroverted. They wanted something quite bold," says Dance

LIGHT

The deck on the first floor acts as an important light source. But increased light was also achieved by removing many of the sheds from the rear garden, which is now completely unencumbered.

MATERIALS

Like the corrugated steel, the internal materials are simple. The kitchen features timber cupboards, also painted in bright red. The timber used for windows and joinery came from plantation timbers. "My clients wanted to use sustainable materials wherever possible."

FURNITURE

The house is simply furnished. Some of the built-in furniture was designed by Dance. The main bedroom for example, features a built-in desk that appears integral to the stairs leading to the deck.

ADVICE

Ideally look for the right orientation. But sometimes, it's a matter of manipulating a building so that it works with the natural daylight.

Opposite   *Aerial view from back lane; overall height of barrel vault-shaped addition was reduced to permit existing building to be seen from the street*

Following pages
View of addition from back lane

This terrace home, located on the city fringe, features an unadorned façade. Built in the 19th century, the house is flanked by modest single- and double-storey homes of the same era. "Apart from a 1970's addition, little had been done to the house. We were quite fortunate that the original front rooms were still relatively intact," says architect Suzanne Dance. ■ Dance's clients, a couple with a teenage child, were keen to create two living zones, one for themselves, the other for their daughter. To achieve this, the original two front rooms on the first floor were retained for the daughter's use. One room is used as her bedroom, the other as her study. To create the parental zone: Dance designed an entirely new wing on the first floor and separated it by a deck that links the two. The parents' wing includes the main bedroom, ensuite, study nook and a kitchenette. A second staircase leading from the kitchen to the parents' wing ensures a clear division of space. "The two areas are quite independent. It means that everyone has their own space," says Dance. ■ In contrast to the original brick building, the extension is made of corrugated steel. The curved roofline is punctuated at one end with irregularly shaped windows, clearly outlined with bright red trims. "The barrel vaulted roof is quite typical of many Victorian-style buildings. But the shape was also created to limit the height on the boundaries," says Dance. "You still get a sense of space inside these rooms," says Dance, referring to the ceiling, which is 3.5 metres high at its apex. ■ One of the most important aspects of the house is the deck linking the two zones. As the rear garden is relatively small, only a few square metres, the deck allows the outdoor space to be doubled. The deck also creates a light well in the home, sending shafts of light through the shaped windows. "I was also mindful of improving the ventilation in the house. There's a small deck on the other side of the main bedroom. The windows and doors can be left open on either side to allow for the breeze," says Dance. ■ For Dance, the renovation provides continuity of scale but is a contrast in styles, between the original home and the new work. "The Burra Charter (conservation guidelines used in Australia) encourages new work to stand apart from the original. Sometimes it is about exaggerating the differences to enhance the original," she says. ■

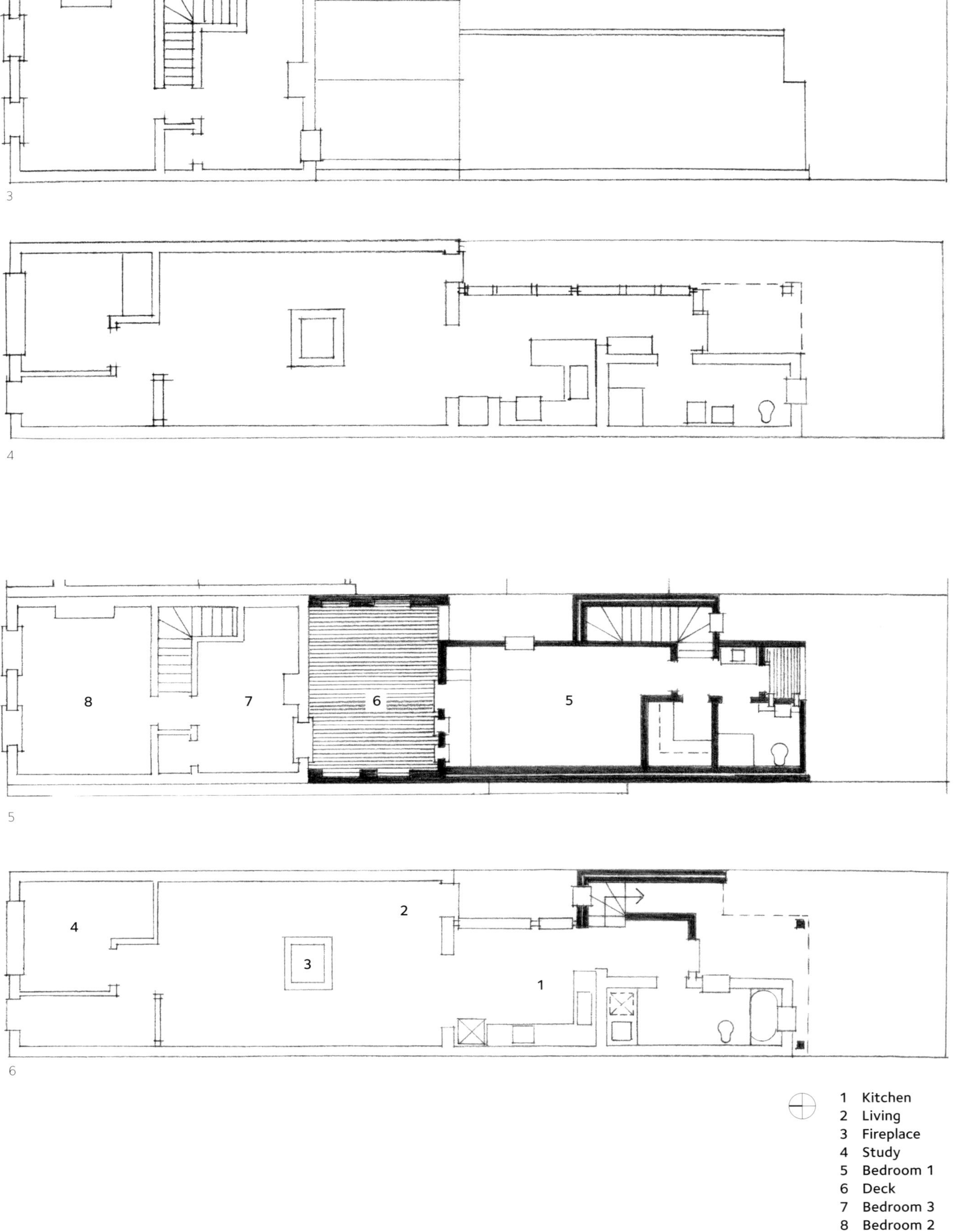

3
4
5
6
1 Kitchen
2 Living
3 Fireplace
4 Study
5 Bedroom 1
6 Deck
7 Bedroom 3
8 Bedroom 2

3   Upper floor plan before
4   Ground floor plan before
5   Upper floor plan after
6   Ground floor plan after
7   View of addition from deck; small random-sized windows form a partial screen
    to the existing house
8   Interior of bedroom looking north to stairway access to deck; new windows are
    either double-glazed or fitted with shutters to insulate against traffic noise

Photography by Andrew Lecky

1 Design of parabolic room at rear reduces impact of building on neighbours and creates a landmark for the area

2 Front façade plays on the theme of the ubiquitous shop front

1

Curvaceous|lines

Hackney, London, UK

Peter Barber Architects

COLOUR

The interior, apart from the timber floors, is white. Barber was more interested in the quality of the light entering the building than the colour of the walls. The only other colour is charcoal grey, which is expressed in the interior, in the steel balustrades and in the window and door frames.

LIGHT

Light is crucial to the success of this design. The courtyard carved out in the centre of the building illuminates the interior spaces. The courtyard also creates a shallow plan rather than the traditional Victorian format of elongated dark spaces.

FURNITURE

The client intends to furnish the townhouse with a mixture of contemporary and antique pieces. Like the work displayed on the gallery walls, they will represent the best of the past and present.

ADVICE

A common mistake made when extending a townhouse is to make the original plan even deeper. This just makes the centre of the house even darker than it was originally. In this project, the lack of light was overcome by inserting a central courtyard. And while it takes away some of the area set aside for living, it has significantly enriched the quality of the spaces.

This townhouse, in London's East End, forms part of a group of shops. Built in about 1850, its charm is partially due to its narrow frontage, approximately 4 metres wide. "In Victorian times, Hackney was quite an affluent suburb. But during the late 20th century, the area fell into decline. In the last few years it has turned into a vibrant neighbourhood," says architect Peter Barber. ■ As the street is a market, most of the neighbouring properties include shops on the ground floor. But while some of these properties retain their original Victorian features, this townhouse was completely derelict. The original shopfront, which is used as a gallery, was retained. The building almost doubled in size with the renovation of a two-bedroom apartment above. ■ Unlike the reserved brick façade, the new extension is punchy, creating a strong architectural gesture to the rear of the property. "The project was designed in collaboration with our client, who describes herself as an 'architecture junkie'," says Barber. "She's interested in the idea of architecture as art, in pure space, light and form." ■ A new steel and glass façade was inserted at ground level. It extends to the first floor with a glass and steel balustrade. Once through the front door, the past is completely left behind. From the street, the only clue to the curvaceous interior comes from the curved reception counter in the gallery. Beyond the gallery's pure white rectilinear walls is a two-storey townhouse, with an open-plan living room under a parabolic barrel vault roof. There are also double-height, open-plan, living and workspaces at the basement and ground-floor levels. ■ To increase the amount of light entering the building, glass bricks were inserted in the timber deck on the first floor. Light also enters from irregularly placed windows in the rear façade and from skylights that were inserted at several points. Even a rear balcony features an open steel grid floor. ■ One of the most important aspects of the design was the new internal courtyard, which allows light to spill into all areas of the building. For Barber, the influences on the design are as diverse as the surrounding buildings. "You could see something of Oscar Niemeyer's work or even Adolf Loos. There's also a strong Arabian vernacular," says Barber of the design that has become a landmark in the area. ■

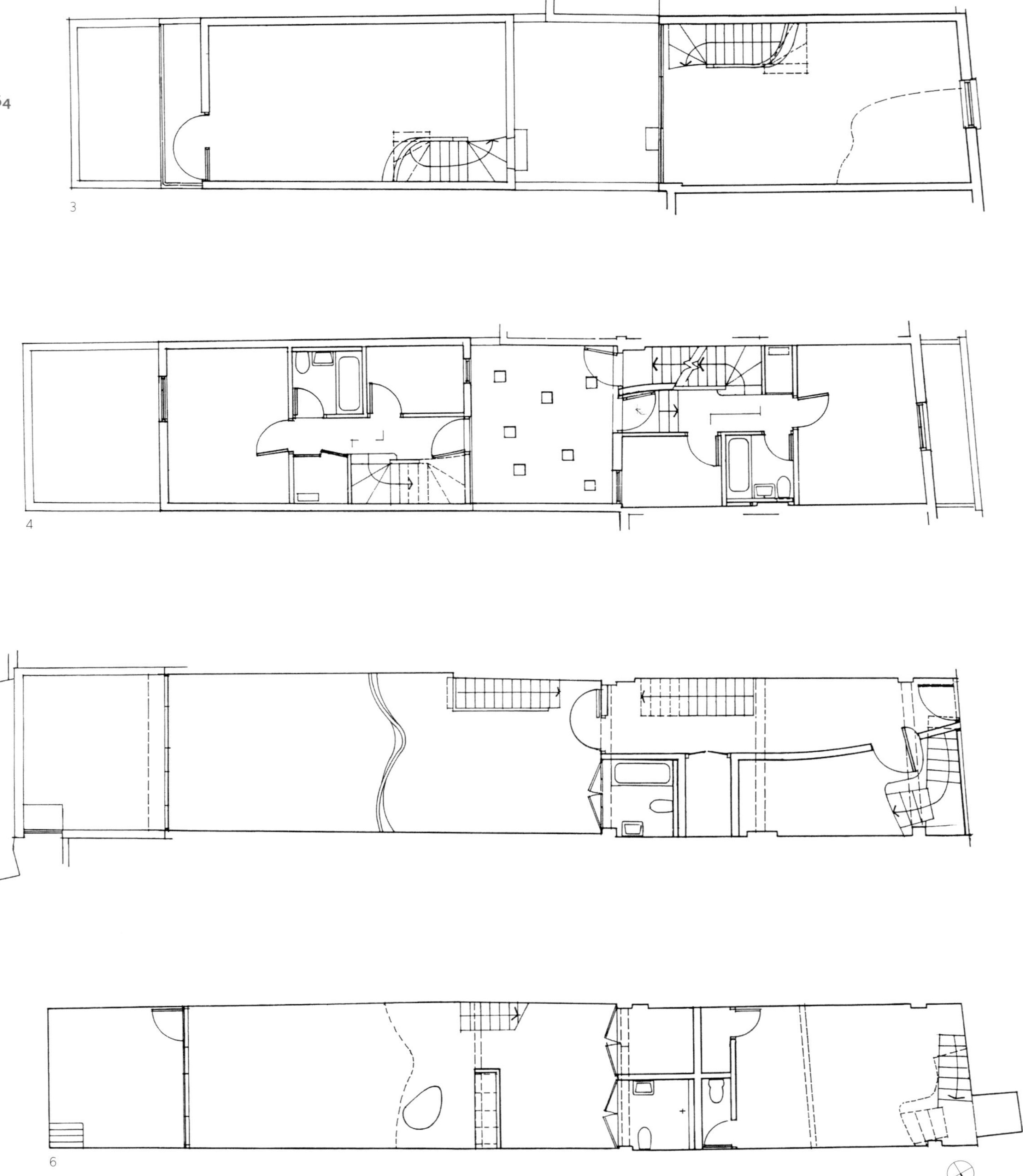

3
4
5
6

3   Second floor plan: open-plan living spaces of upper maisonettes

4   First floor plan: upper maisonettes' bedrooms are separated from courtyard with roof lights

5   Ground floor plan: gallery mezzanine at front; live/work mezzanine at rear

6   Basement plan: gallery space at front; double-height live/work space with private courtyard at rear

7   Central courtyard at first-floor level separates the two upper maisonettes and allows light into an otherwise deep plan

8   View into double-height live/work space from private basement courtyard at rear

9   The window design creates light and shadow play on the curved interior

Photography by Morley von Sternberg

7

8

9

66

1 Front elevation of single-storey terrace (left)

2 Garden and garage door sculptural mechanism with concrete planter above

3 View of rear elevation; slatted garage door ensures privacy while concrete planter adds an aesthetic element

4 Entry hall with view into guest bathroom

Deceptive|from the|street

Sydney, New South Wales, Australia

Stephen Varady Architecture

LIGHT

The stairwell was conceived as a lightshaft. A large picture window at the top of the stairs draws light into the living spaces on the ground floor. Highlight windows in the main bathroom also bring light into what were once dark pockets in the house. A courtyard between the living area and second bedroom allows light to filter into the new wing and the original part of the house.

COLOUR

The client requested an all-white house. As her daughters are painters, she wanted a neutral backdrop on which to display their work. She also wanted a blank canvas to display her own collection of objects and artefacts. Varady was keen to add some drama to the house, which was achieved by painting the walls and ceiling of the staircase a bright red, and laying bright red carpet on the treads. "The light from the staircase creates a pink glow in the living spaces," says Varady.

MATERIALS

The new wing is a timber frame construction, built on a concrete slab. While the original front two rooms of the house were retained, timber floorboards had to be reinstated as a result of rot. The new living areas feature polished concrete floors and simple joinery. White Marblo was used for the kitchen bench tops.

ADVICE

Engage someone with vision. These houses can be quite daunting to renovate. You need to be able to make the space feel considerably larger than it actually is. It's about manipulating spaces and leading your eye to the furthest points of the property.

This row house looks relatively small from the street. Only 5 metres wide, it has the feel of a cottage rather than a large home. However, the house opens up to reveal large and generous spaces, high on drama. ■ The house originally consisted of two front rooms, a living room and a kitchen and dining area. A bathroom had been tacked onto the kitchen. While the front two rooms of the house were retained, beyond a new pivotal door in the corridor the home appears completely new, including a second-storey addition. The house now features four bedrooms, (two upstairs), an open-plan living, kitchen and dining area, together with ensuites upstairs and a separate laundry and bathroom downstairs. To create garden views, a courtyard garden was designed on each side of the new living spaces. ■ Unlike many terrace renovations that position a new staircase in line with the existing corridor, the staircase was located on the other side of the living area. "People have to walk around the living area to reach the staircase. But this allows them to explore the entire space rather than just moving in an upward direction from the front door," says Varady. The staircase, which features a picture window, was also positioned to draw additional light into the living spaces. The landing at the top of the stairs has a glass floor, increasing the level of light in the home. ■ The bedrooms upstairs are large and private, each with its own bathroom. To achieve a greater sense of space, the main bedroom and ensuite 'borrow' space and light from each other through the use of a clear glass wall, allowing two modest sized spaces to feel much larger than they actually are. ■ To complement the two street frontages, Varady designed a sensitive rear façade, while incorporating a garage door and gate. Council regulations required some visibility to be maintained from the street into the rear garden, so the garage door was designed with a series of angled blades that give a greater sense of openness between the garden and the street, while at the same time blocking any view into the rear of the house. ■

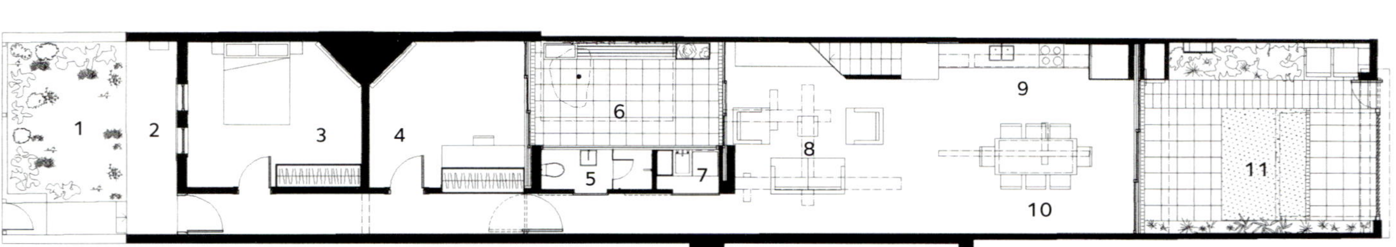

1 Garden
2 Porch
3 Bedroom 1
4 Bedroom 2
5 Bathroom
6 Courtyard
7 Laundry
8 Living
9 Kitchen
10 Dining
11 Garden
12 Storage
13 Bedroom 3
14 Bathroom
15 Ensuite
16 Bedroom 4

5   First floor plan

6   Ground floor plan

7   Sculpted ceiling of living, dining and kitchen with sun shining through stairwell

8   Kitchen

9   Glass floor to first-floor hallway

10   Wash of sunlight down stairwell to kitchen

11   First-floor hallway

12   Red stairwell from ground floor

13   Red stairwell from first floor

9

11

13

69

12

10

15

16

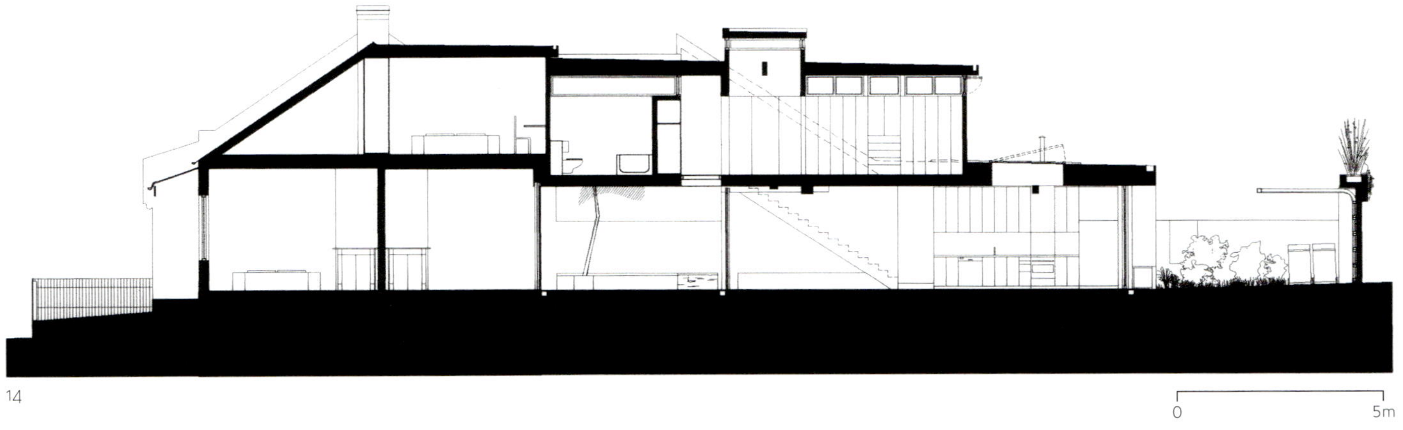

14

17

18

14 *Section*
15 *Bedroom 4 and ensuite*
16 *Bedroom 3 and bathroom*
17 *Bathroom*
18 *Detail of ensuite sliding glass door, shower, light and windows*

Photography by Stephen Varady

1

2

Desert|spa|retreat

Tucson, Arizona, USA

Ibarra Rosano Design Architects

COLOUR

The use of colour is restrained and reserved for points of accent and focus, to conceptually achieve the light and spatial qualities of a cloud resting on a hill. Soft hues of blue and green represent the vegetation and water elements.

MATERIALS

The approach was one of reduction and simplification. The palette of material textures is simple and minimal, intended to bounce light off soft textures, which helps unify the spaces.

FURNITURE

The furniture is selected and designed to complement the restraint and simplicity of the space while adding comfort and utility by unassuming placement.

ADVICE

"Out of clutter, find simplicity; from discord, find harmony; in the middle of difficulty lies opportunity." – Albert Einstein

3

1   Side entrance and driveway before
2   Material choice and composition create a serene entry
3   The sun rises on the south porch

This transformation began as a simple request for a bathroom remodel. The owners wanted to achieve the contemplative feel of a modern spa or boutique hotel, in stark contrast to the haphazard flow and disparate finishes of their existing residence. ■ The existing structure was a modest 1940's brick house with an awkward and poorly detailed 1990's addition. After understanding the level of design the owners wanted for the bathrooms, it was clear that the entire house would need to be transformed. Although a tear-down was briefly contemplated, the architects ultimately decided to remodel the 3515-square-foot home, adding a mere 35 square feet in the form of a new shower. ■ One key to transforming the house was in the removal of the large, poorly built, load-bearing stone fireplace that dominated and bisected the main living spaces. Once it was demolished and the roof re-supported, the opening became a perfect opportunity for a large skylight that now fills the once-trapped living spaces with daylight. With the main living room freed from the constraints of the fireplace, some of that floor area was used to enlarge the master bathroom and closet. Removing the dividing wall between the closet and bathroom created an open and light-filled space for dressing and bathing. ■ The original seldom-used 'front door' was on the south side of the living room, but access was incompatible with the natural sloped terrain and vehicular access to the site. Responding to the natural flow towards the house on its hilltop site, the architects chose to keep the side entrance as the primary entry and created a dramatic concrete and beach-pebble parking plaza between the new carport and entry. ■ Several new small courtyards and patios throughout the house create a feeling of connection to the exterior while providing shelter and privacy. The area that had once been an awkward circular dirt driveway adjacent to the study and guest room became a serene courtyard with a fountain, a small square of grass, a single tree and a rectilinear opening that perfectly frames the city skyline. The inclusion of a tiny courtyard around the glass and tile shower addition on the east side of the house allows the bather to feel as if he or she is outside while still surrounded by privacy. ■ A new blue glass tiled and terrazzo-like plastered pool provides a dramatic focus, with the desired spa-like feel, for the interior spaces. A pair of 'floating' concrete bridges links the main deck to a master bedroom deck and linear outdoor fireplace. ■ After more than a year of living in the dust of remodeling, the owners love the idea that they can invite their out-of-town friends and family to their very own spa-like retreat in the desert. ■

74

4

17

16
5
3
4
1
2
6
15
14
9
8
13
11
7
18
12
10
19

1 Entry
2 Kitchen
3 Pantry
4 Powder room
5 Laundry
6 TV room
7 Dining
8 Living
9 Office
10 West bedroom
11 West bathroom
12 East bedroom
13 East bathroom
14 Master bedroom
15 Master bathroom
16 Pool
17 Carport
18 Sunroom
19 Porch

5

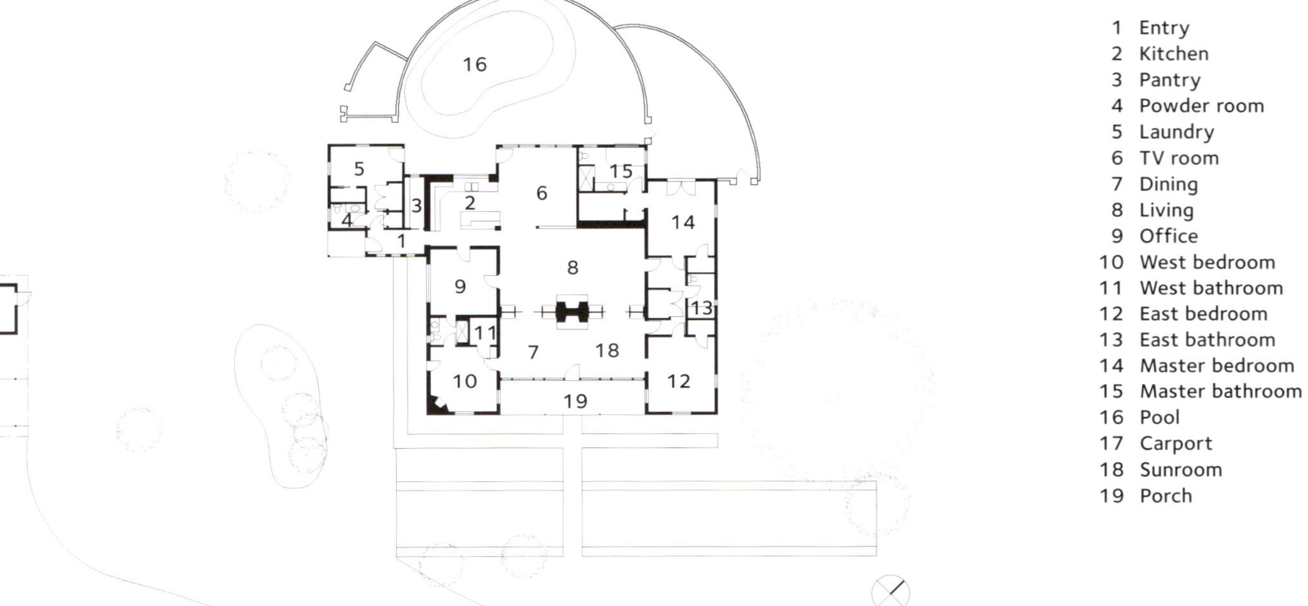

4 *Floor plan before*

5 *Night view of the city lights from the living room*

6 *Dining room before*

7 *The skylight bathes the living and dining rooms
with balanced light*

8 *Floor plan after*

1	Entry hall	14	East bedroom
2	Kitchen	15	East bathroom
3	Pantry	16	Shower courtyard
4	Powder room	17	Master bedroom
5	Laundry	18	Master bath/closet
6	TV room	19	Outdoor fireplace
7	Dining room	20	Dining patio
8	Living room	21	Pool
9	Office	22	Trash enclosure
10	West bedroom	23	South deck
11	West bathroom	24	Carport
12	West courtyard	25	Entry plaza
13	East hall		

9   *East bathroom before*

10   *Master bathroom before*

11   *Living and dining rooms, seen from the kitchen*

12   *The floating vanity straddles the bathing and dressing sides of the master bathroom*

13   *Custom outdoor fireplace, seen from the master bathroom*

14   *The east bathroom features a glass-enclosed shower in a private yard*

9

10

11

12

13

14

15

16

17

15 A meditative garden space with a view of the city in the distance
16 Deep water, blue tile and plaster visually cool the yard
17 Pool with cantilevered bridge unites public and private yards
18 Pool and backyard before

Photography by Bill Timmerman

18

79

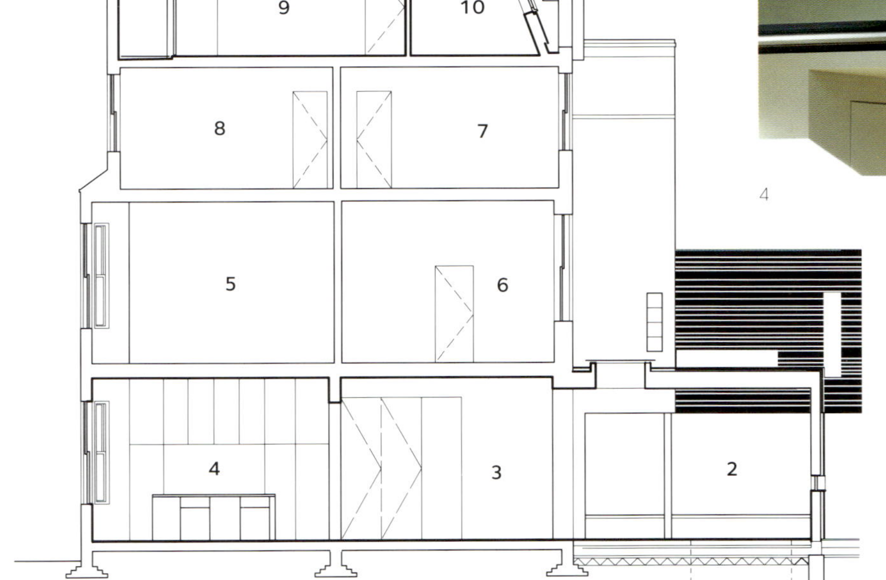

1 Wine cellar
2 Family room
3 Dining
4 Kitchen
5 Sitting room
6 Master bedroom
7 Bedroom
8 Bedroom
9 Bedroom
10 Bathroom

The Ultimate Urban Makeover

Designed|for the 21st|century

London, UK
Robert Dye Associates

COLOUR

The main use of colour is the black stain to the exterior. This was used to give sharpness and clearly define the volume of the timber boxes. But the extension does not dominate the overall context of the rear terrace and garden. The colours used for the interior are considerably lighter, including grey natural stone and oak for the benches and floor on the ground level.

LIGHT

The round skylight near the junction of the extension to the main house allows significant light into what has become the middle of a deep-plan house. The rear façade features large glass sliding doors and has high clerestories above. Sandblasted glass has been used for the shower, bathroom and toilet doors to borrow light into the stairwell. There is also a new skylight at roof level, as well as a mansard window to let further additional light into the stairwell.

VENTILATION

All the skylights have trickle vents. The clerestory windows over the family room's bi-fold doors allow evening ventilation without violating security. The new wing has also improved circulation in the home, with the ground floor now a single open-plan space.

FURNITURE

The furniture was selected by the owners with the architect's guidance, sometimes, as in the family room, to fit specific niches. Furniture is mainly contemporary on the ground floor, supplemented by a few antique pieces from the family's travels.

ADVICE

Identify the opportunities to let light into the areas of the main house that become sunken into the plan. And try to achieve a hierarchy and balance of spaces by allowing a reading of the full width of the plan.

1   *View of rear at project commencement*
2   *Section*
3   *View of rear at project completion*
4   *Bathroom 'box' hovering within living space*

Located on the southern fringes of London's Hampstead Heath, this early Edwardian, four-storey house (circa 1900) had experienced several renovations. These included an awkward 1970's extension at the rear of the ground floor, extending uncomfortably into the rear garden. "The interior had seen many attempts to decorate and 'contemporise' the house, mixing up the eras," says architect Robert Dye. ■ While the house wasn't considered significant by local authorities, it was part of an intact streetscape, featuring rows of Victorian and Edwardian homes. "This house is in a conservation area. We had no intention of altering the façade. It was the interior that required significant work," says Dye, who recalls the lack of period features. "The only things we inherited were some original high skirting boards and cornices in some of the rooms," he adds. ■ The owners' brief was to add two bedrooms, create a new family bathroom, a children's bathroom and a new informal living area that would link to the rear garden. "One of the owners wanted to be able to see the garden from the front door. The other requested the exterior be brought into the interior, to recall spaces he had experienced as a child in a 'Corbusier' house in India," says Dye. ■ The first-floor front sitting room and the second-floor bedrooms were restored. Although the kitchen and dining areas remain on the ground floor, they have been completely redesigned. The new family area is an integral part of the garden (sliding folding doors allow unhindered access to the garden). The renovation is characterised by two intersecting cubes, one containing the main bathroom on the first floor, the other the family room at ground level. Clad in black-stained treated Russian redwood and featuring generous glazed openings that frame specific garden views, the playful extension creates a lighter side to the home's original Edwardian façade. ■ Certain clues and lines through the house link the two periods. The skirting heights, for example, have been maintained and drawn through from the older to the newer areas of the house. "There was also a conscious game played with the ceiling heights of the existing house," says Dye, who was keen to create an ethereal atmosphere in the home. As a consequence, polished vanity tops reflect the sky, as do the pale heated limestone floors. ■

5

5 Intersection detail of interlocked boxes
6 Main living space fully opened to terrace
7 Openings to garden, terrace and sky from main living space
8 Third floor plan
9 Second floor plan
10 First floor plan
11 Ground floor plan
12 Slot window from bathroom to rear garden landscape
13 Sandblasted screen and protected tree at end of bathroom box

Photography by Sue Barr (3,4,6,7,13)
courtesy Robert Dye Associates (1,5,12)

6

7

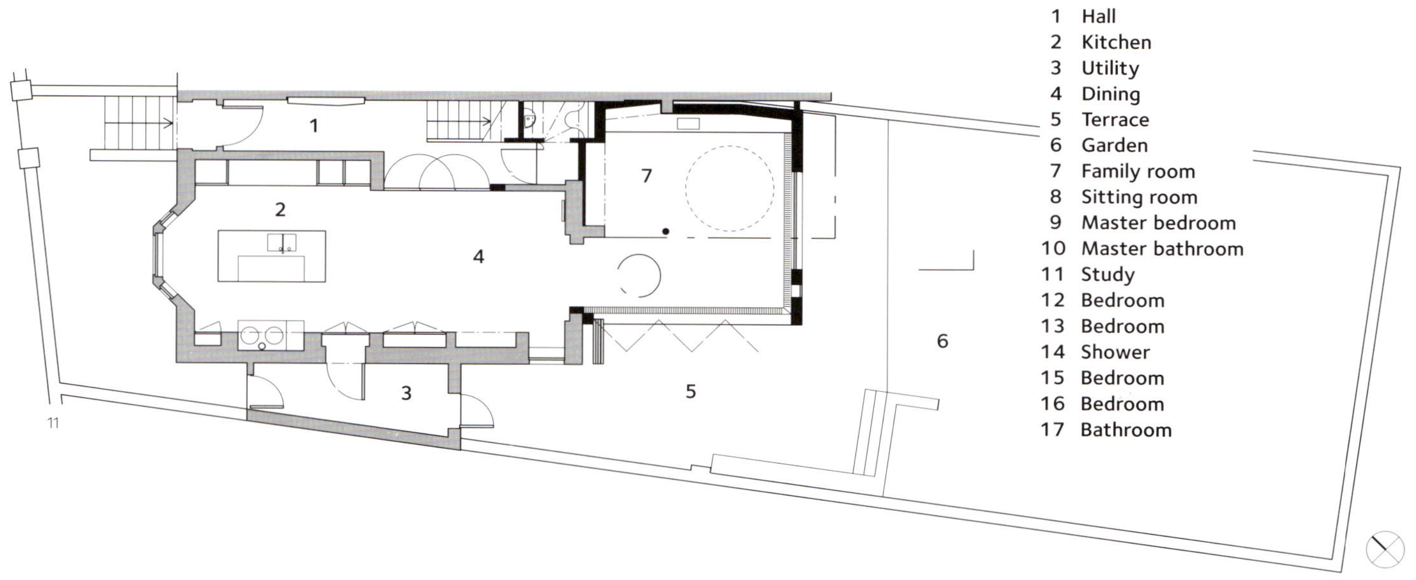

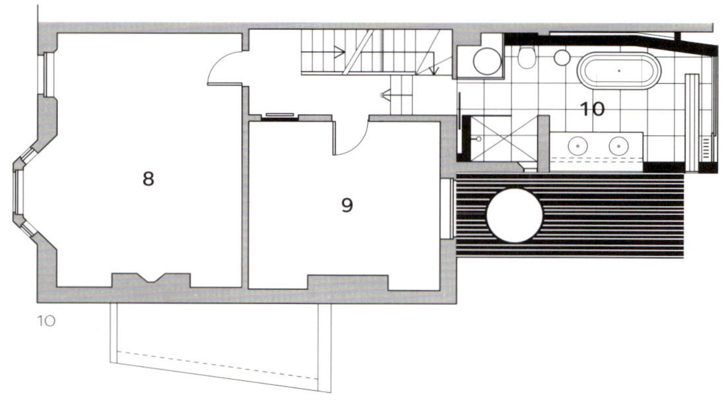
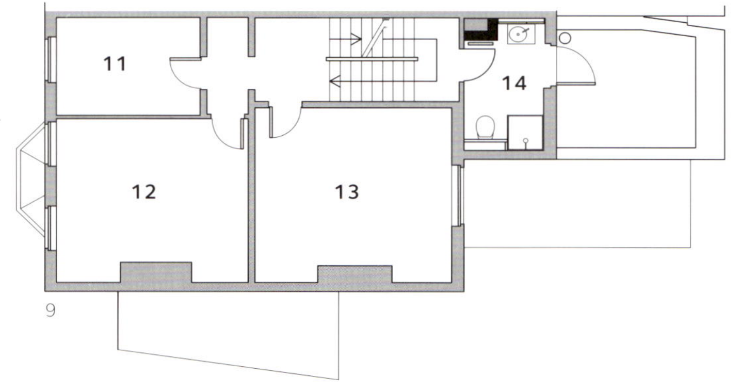
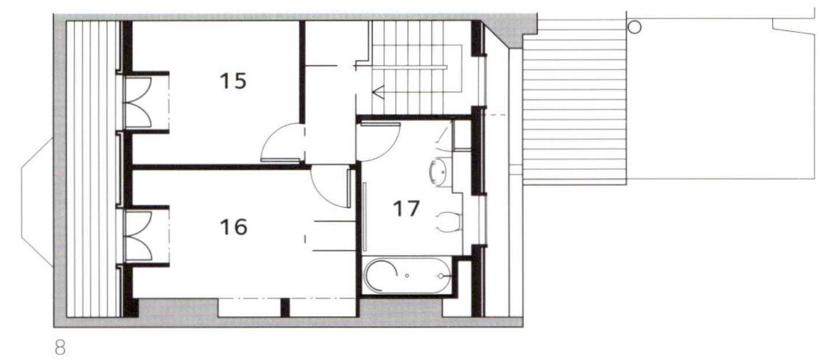

1 Hall
2 Kitchen
3 Utility
4 Dining
5 Terrace
6 Garden
7 Family room
8 Sitting room
9 Master bedroom
10 Master bathroom
11 Study
12 Bedroom
13 Bedroom
14 Shower
15 Bedroom
16 Bedroom
17 Bathroom

A different side

Melbourne, Victoria, Australia
McBride Charles Ryan Architecture + Interior Design

Colour

The original rooms in the house were restored, with the walls and corridor painted white. The new wing also features white walls. The main interior colour comes from the orange curtain that frames the kitchen and living areas. Additional colour appears in the rear façade, which includes pine plywood, stained lime green to capture the colour of the first buds of the mature ash tree in the rear garden.

Materials

A variety of materials was used for the new wing, including a green-black Colorbond that wraps around the new extension and deep messmate-clad eaves. "The relationship of the house to the garden is always crucial in our work," says McBride.

Circulation

To avoid the one long central passage synonymous with terrace homes, a new staircase was placed to one side of the living area, freeing up the large continuous open-plan area in the new wing.

Light

Natural light was brought into the house from both sides of the house and from the rear garden. Courtyard spaces frame the new living areas and light filters into the space from above via a skylight in the kitchen. Two large picture windows were installed at both ends of the corridor leading to the children's bedrooms, allowing light and views to the first floor.

Advice

"When you are renovating a period home, invert the design from the original configuration. For us, the new work is about configuring the internal and external spaces simultaneously and treating them as one," says McBride.

Set back from a wrought-iron front fence, this tuck-pointed Victorian house is neatly aligned with the other period homes in the street. The contemporary extension to the house is a courtyard style with rooms surrounding an internal courtyard. "We wanted to bring in the light and use all the spaces around the house," says architect Rob McBride. ■ The extension to the house is made of Colorbond, lime-stained plywood and aluminium, and features deep spotted gum eaves. One of the rear walls is in black bamboo. The chosen colours not only create a different style to the house, but reflect the colours of an established ash tree, positioned to one side of the property. Spotted gum timber also features in the courtyard leading from the kitchen and living area. "We wanted to create a natural outlook throughout the house, whether it is polished stones or black bamboo. It was important to make the garden feel part of the house," says interior designer Debbie-Lyn Ryan. ■ The house was designed for a couple with three small children. And while they appreciated the home's Victorian charm, the original spaces were insufficient. "We wanted something that was warm, but also had a certain energy," says Gill, the owner. "We also wanted our own space," she adds. The original front two rooms were retained as the parents' domain; one is used as a formal lounge, the other as the main bedroom, ensuite and dressing area. ■ Past the decorative Victorian archway in the central passage (used as a gallery), there is a jolt to the present, with the corniced ceiling sliced by a new sliding door and by the lower ceiling height in the new wing. From a confined hallway, the house opens to a new living room, central kitchen and dining area, set a few steps below the main living area. ■ The change between the old and new is made even more dramatic by a billowing orange curtain that frames the sliding doors to the courtyard. "The colour was inspired by the original Victorian leadlight that surrounds the front door. I still remember first seeing the intensity of the red reflection on the timber floors," says Ryan, who saw the design as being quite theatrical from the outset. And while the original part of the house remains as a single storey, the rear of the house includes a second level, comprising the children's bedrooms, bathroom and play area. ■ The design provided the setting for the owner's sculpture collection. A sculpture by Greg Johns features prominently in the back garden, outside the dining area. Another sculpture by Peter McLisky is positioned in its

Opposite *View from backyard dining room through to north courtyard*

(continued)

10

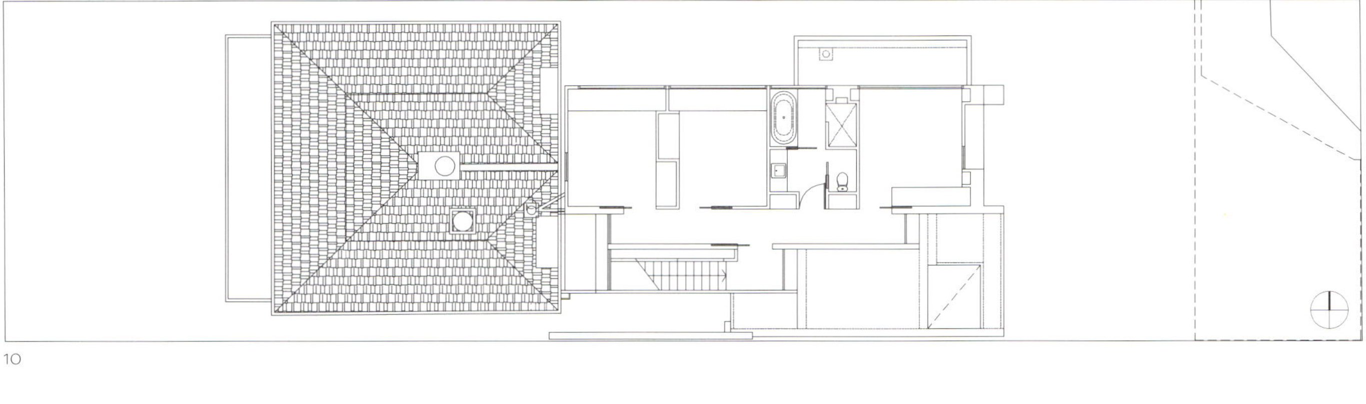

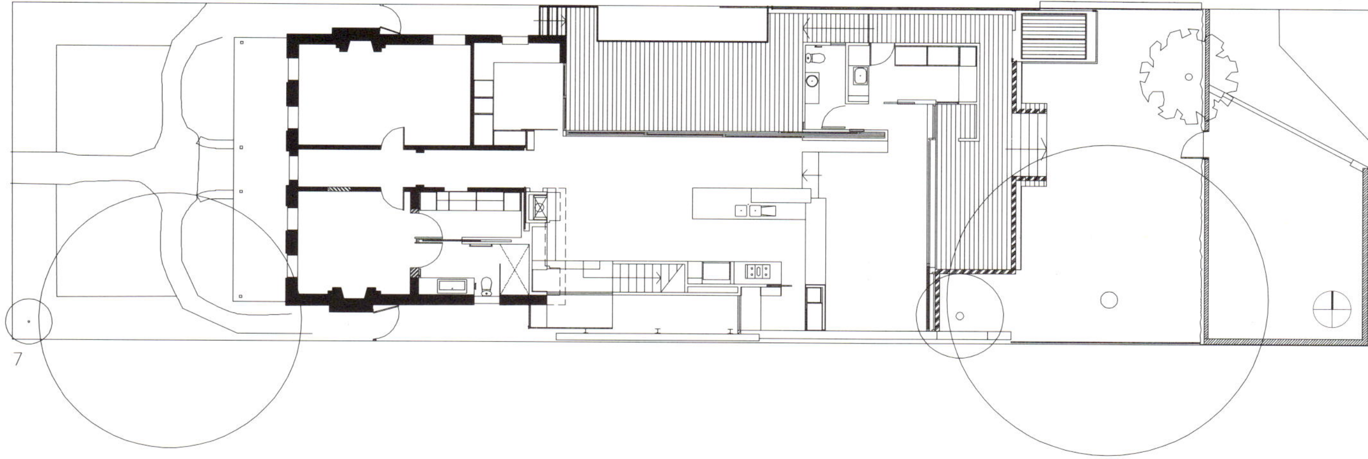

7 Ground floor plan
8 Rear garden
9 New living area
10 First floor plan

Following pages
Overview of new living area, central kitchen
and dining area

Photography by Louis Petruccelli

8

9

The Ultimate Urban Makeover

own niche at the base of the stairs, leading to the three children's bedrooms upstairs. As Ryan says, "we wanted to extend the views into the garden from several angles. The courtyard acts as another room." ■

2   Orange curtain framing courtyard
3   View from front door
4   View towards original spaces
5   North courtyard
6   West elevation

1   *Built in 1928, cottage and detached garage are Tudor-style 'storybook' structures crafted in stucco and stone with metal casement windows and concrete shingles*

2   *Side view of cottage showing informal entry; the unusual depth of the gabled roof is visible from this angle*

1

Double|take

Croton–on–Hudson, New York, USA

Philip Tusa, Architect

LIGHT/VENTILATION

The removal of partitions created open spaces within. Large glazed areas take advantage of diagonal views and unobstructed sunlight.

COLOUR

In the studio, the colour palette expresses contrast; grey for the walkway and black for the desks and linear elements. A white translucent pleated shade controls solar glare for the large work surface. The same colour palette is used in the cottage.

ADVICE

Structures such as garages or workshops are ideal candidates for conversion into working and living spaces. Because buildings from earlier periods in general did not have very large windows, maximising views by installing large windows, where possible, will take advantage of a site's geography and provide improved ventilation.

This project is a renovation of a cottage and detached garage. Built in 1928, the buildings are located on a site that slopes towards the Hudson River, offering superb views. The garage was converted into an architect's studio while the cottage underwent a complete makeover that transformed it into a cosy living space. ■ The garage was converted into a studio for architect Philip Tusa. Its fine craftsmanship and textured elements were considered when the renovation process began: the heavily textured stucco and metal casements were preserved; open-riser stairs were installed and some partitions were removed to open up areas both inside and out. ■ Despite the modest size of the garage, its deep roof gables allow the architectural elements to scale to a second-storey height. Careful management of space allows the inclusion of a stairway to a landing leading to a desk. Additionally the vertical bookshelves, lateral pin-up wall and linear railing are interwoven to integrate the efficiency of this small volume. The white bookshelves are stacked to a height of 5 metres and a new opening on the side of the building was created. The metal casement windows match the existing windows, the garage door and the new side opening. ■ The cottage had a stairway created by removing the existing wood risers to create an open-riser system of stairs that allows a more open view. To maximise the open view, new oculus openings, both as windows in the entry doors and the clear opening between stairway and dining room, were created. Built-in seating, beds and bookshelves throughout were custom-made. ■ Although the renovation of the cottage and garage studio transformed two separate buildings, similar materials and colours were used. All interior walls and ceilings are painted in white gloss-finish, floors are carpeted with varying shades of grey and black counters and several wainscot-height surfaces and floor moulding add contrast and highlight selected shapes. Colour is added with art and craft such as Indonesian puppets, African sculptures and Indian fabric for pillows. ■

2

3

4

3 *View from kitchen into living room/entry and formal front doorway; stairway is to the right*

4 *Detail of oculus viewed through open-riser stair treads towards side entry*

5 *Looking down stairway to side entry with view into child's bedroom; bed is built in to the 'knee wall' space*

6 *Garage studio features stairway that leads to a catwalk to reach an additional desk and provides access to double-height bookshelves*

7 *View of garage studio showing entry and conference area to rear*

8 *Detailed view of catwalk railing with upper-level desk beyond*

6

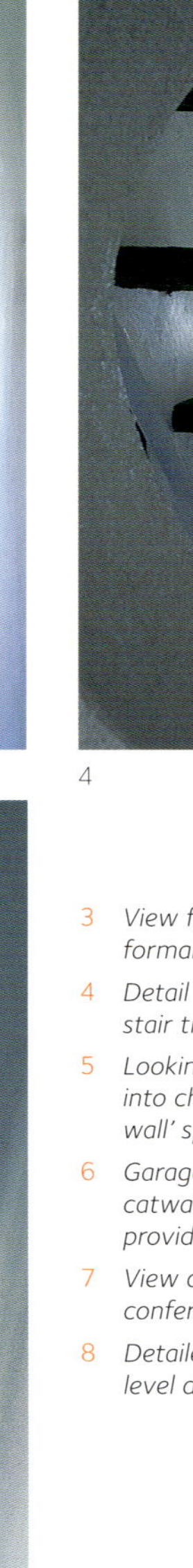

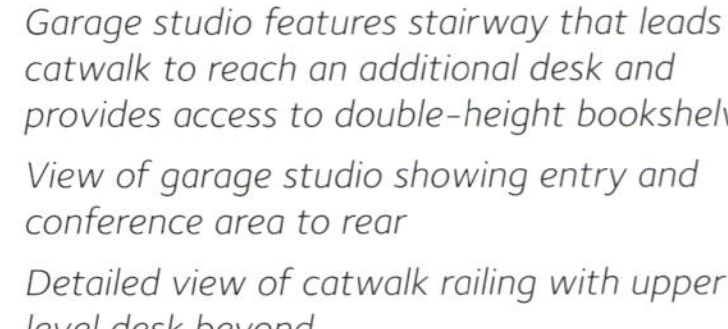

5

9

9   *View of living room looking towards side entry; fireplace with mirror mantelpiece to left*

10   *View towards dining room from kitchen; entry to basement stairway, with the oculus opening beyond, is to the left*

11   *Doorway to master bedroom reveals bed, banquette window seat and casement window with a view of the Hudson River*

Photography by Paul Warchol (1–5, 9–11)
Peter Paige (6–8)

The Ultimate Urban Makeover

1 *Carriage house/garage anchors the backyard garden*
2 *Built in 1896, the home was in disrepair*
3 *Twenty layers of paint were stripped from the house*
4 *Designed for a sculptor, the house was lovingly restored by the architect-owner*
5 *The Greek goddess Athena is depicted in the Melchers carving*

Dutch|delight

Detroit, Michigan, USA

McIntosh Poris Associates

COLOUR

A meticulous restoration of the original Melchers hand-carved details was achieved by consulting historic photos of the house. The exterior wood clapboard was stripped of 20 layers of paint. The colours used on the exterior include colonial yellow with a cream trim accented with green tones to highlight details of the restored carvings. A century of paint was stripped from the ceiling, walls and ornamentations to reveal original, hand-carved details. A blue porcelain finish completes the walls above the wainscoting, accentuating the hues of the Delft tile surrounding the fireplace.

FURNITURE

The house comes to life with a superb collection of antique pieces chosen to maintain the original tones set in the 19th century. The music room features an ornately carved Jacobean cupboard and a 1920s-era Steck player baby grand piano; two 1940s-era leather lounge chairs balance the room. Off the stair hall is the original, restored marble butler's sink.

ADVICE

You don't own an historic house – you're just a caretaker. Learn to recognise the pure quality of what was there. Making the home historically accurate is challenging and fun. Trying to figure out how things were done in the first place, then translating it into today's methods is really gratifying.

5

The original, Dutch-influenced home was built and designed in 1896 by Gari Melchers for his father, celebrated Detroit-based artist and sculptor Julius Melchers. Architect Douglas McIntosh purchased the home in 2001, and spent the next five years lovingly restoring it. The renovated three-storey structure includes a foyer, music room, morning room, sunroom, four new bathrooms, kitchen, dining room, master suite, three bedrooms, family room, balcony and loft. ■ The restoration and renovation project involved a complete overhaul of internal mechanics, restructuring of dilapidated areas, new construction, and detailed restoration based on historic photographs. ■ By 2001, most parts of the house had been abandoned, with the back wing nearly collapsed. After comprehensively revamping all of the mechanical, electrical and plumbing systems, the back wing was lifted off its original foundations and reinforced with structural steel. A new cedar and copper roof replaced three others that had been layered over the original pine roof. ■ Interior construction required establishing sectional relief where there originally was none. Three bedrooms evolved into the master suite on the second floor. A revision of the original sunroom created a two-storey sunroom with views of the newly created courtyard and carriage house. A large family room was created on the third floor, where three bedrooms once existed, and a new third-floor balcony replaced unfinished attic space. A fourth-level loft overlooks the third-floor space and completes the complex relationship within the restored structure. ■ The dining room's design includes the restoration of the original corner cupboards and 400-year-old Delft tile imported from Holland. An intimate Dutch vestibule – complete with antique Dutch courting mirrors flanking the split Dutch door – stands at the elegantly carved grand entrance and stair hall. An Art Moderne prismatic light fixture from the 1930s graces the entry foyer. ■ Outside, a new carriage house functions as garage, courtyard and storage facility, taking advantage of the alley access to the home. The space comprises two symmetrical wings flanking a sunken courtyard. Each wing accommodates one car, with a storage loft located above. The connecting space between the two garages was designed to be a summer kitchen that can extend to the courtyard, which doubles as an alfresco dining room. ■

6 *Photo-murals by a local artist enhance the historic theme*

7 *A player piano and Jacobean cupboard enhance the music room*

8 *Second floor plan*

9 *Antique lavatory door in the master bathroom was salvaged from a church confessional*

10 *First floor plan*

11 *Ground floor plan*

1 Great room
2 Archive room
3 Loft above stair, open to great room below
4 Sitting room
5 Mechanical room
6 Open to sitting room below

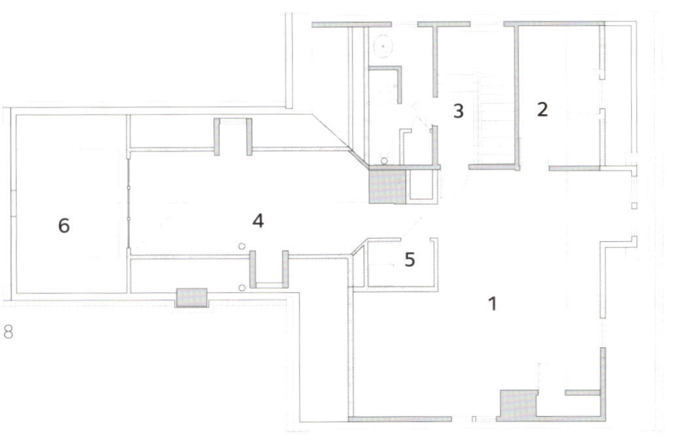

8

9

1 Sitting room
2 Master bedroom
3 Guest bedroom
4 Dressing room
5 Master bathroom
6 Card room
7 Sun room

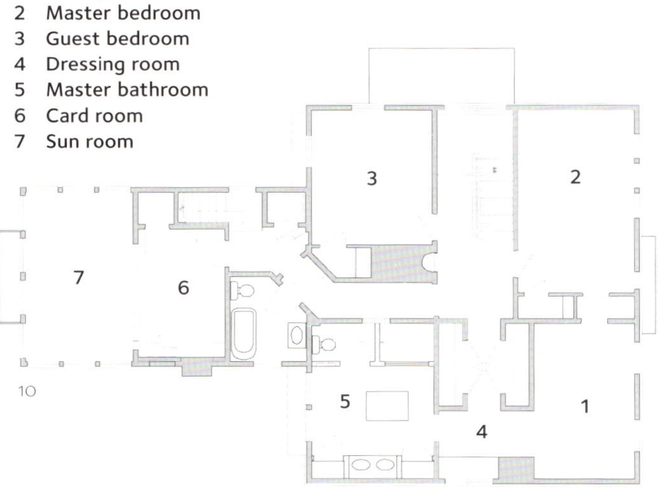

10

1 Vestibule
2 Foyer
3 Living room
4 Dining room
5 Butler's pantry
6 Kitchen
7 Sun room
8 Rear stair
9 Powder room
10 Library
11 Front stair
12 Music room

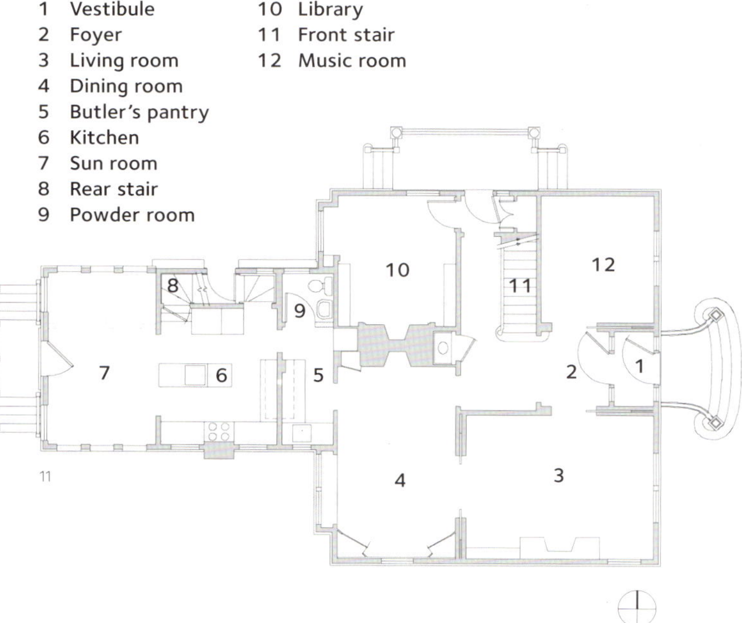

11

12 *Range area includes a Melchers sculpture and antique Delft tiles*
13 *Sunny entryway echoes the yellow exterior*
14 *Dining room features built-in window seat and carved mouldings*

Photography by Kevin Bauman (1,4–7,13,14)
Justin Maconochie (9,12)

The Ultimate Urban Makeover

13

14

1 New work is not visible from street frontage
2 Rear of house during demolition; existing roof form, which was continued in new work, is visible
3 View of rear façade from garden space

Expressing|the|light

Melbourne, Victoria, Australia
NMBW Architecture Studio

Light

As the house suffered from a lack of natural light, two new skylights were incorporated in the home, one over the new living area, the other at the perimeter of the new wing. "We wanted the materials to reflect the light and to allow the light to become animated, whether during the day or at night," says McLean. Lights were installed behind the timber trusses to accentuate the form of the roof.

Colour

Walls in the original house and in the new wing are white. The only additional colour appears in the limed plywood used for the staircase and the joinery, both in the kitchen and in built-in cupboards in the living area. The frames of the doors to the back garden are timber, stained black to allow them to be recessive to the garden aspect. "We were more interested in the materials changing the quality of the light than using colour in the interior," says McLean.

Circulation

"It's important to understand how the house worked originally as well as how it needs to function now. Light wasn't an important issue in the Victorian period. But the qualities of light in a house are as important as how the new spaces are configured," says McLean. While this house has a certain linearity due to the dimensions of the site, the spaces are now continuous and free flowing. "Before, the house was just chopped up; each room was quite pokey".

Advice

There isn't a formula for renovating terraces. Each one is different. You need to understand how the terrace works, whichever city it's located in," says Bertram.

This row house is one of a pair in a street that contains a variety of narrow homes, dating from several periods. Despite their different vintages, all homes have relatively narrow frontages; this one is just under 5 metres wide. ■ While the inner-city location suited the owners, a couple with two young children, the original cottage, built in the late 1800s, was inappropriate. The house originally comprised two rooms at the front; a number of rooms were added in later decades. A large freestanding fireplace, located between the living and kitchen areas still remained. "The last renovation was in the 1970s. The walls containing the fireplace were removed, probably to give the place a more open-plan feel," says architect Lucinda McLean. ■ The three front rooms of the original house were retained and are used as bedrooms. And as the house featured a high-pitched roof, there was sufficient room to add an attic that can be used as a study/guest bedroom. Because the long corridor wasn't wide enough to place a staircase, a new staircase, accessed by a doorway from the main corridor, was inserted between two of the front bedrooms. This sculptural staircase, clad in limed plywood, is expressed in the two bedrooms on the ground floor. One of the children's beds is even positioned in the nook of the staircase wall. ■ The large freestanding fireplace was removed in the renovation, allowing an unimpeded view into the back garden. An entirely new wing, comprising the kitchen, dining area and living area, was also added. While the new form follows the shape of the existing steel roof, the new footprint extends an extra metre to a side boundary. The extra space allows for a galley-style kitchen and features the same limed-plywood as used in the staircase. ■ While the line of the new roof follows the original, the last 900 millimetres of the new roof is clad in translucent fibreglass. "We wanted to expose the timber roof trusses and to bring additional light into the house," says McLean, referring to the lightwell formed at the perimeter of the new living area. To maximise this light, a long stainless bench was inserted adjacent to the kitchen, complete with a canteen-style window that links to the garden. The new wing shows an understanding not only of the original form of the terrace, but an appreciation of the other period homes in the street. As architect Nigel Bertram says, "We didn't just see this home in isolation to the others in the street. This house is part of a larger system, in a broader environment." ■

4

5

6

4   Detail of fibreglass cladding and frameless side windows over kitchen bench
5   Entrance to new attic stair from existing hallway
6   New stair wraps around existing bedroom walls
7   Sections
8   Attic plan (left); ground floor plan (right)
9   Kitchen alcove
10 New kitchen bench viewed from rear

Photography by Lucinda McLean

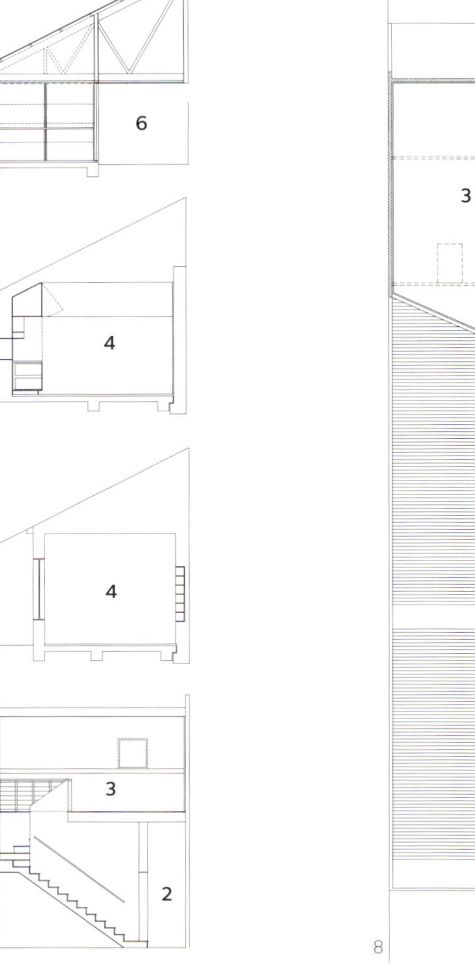
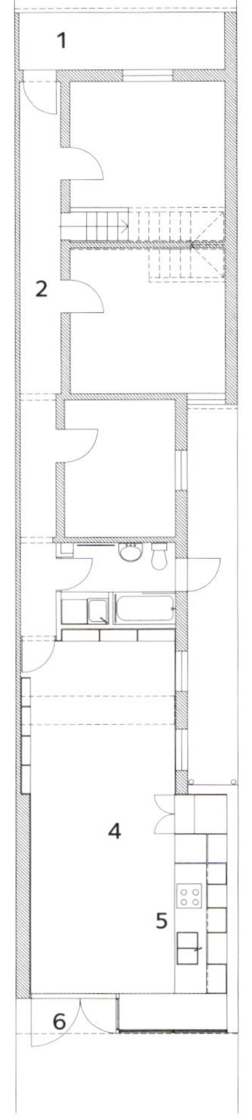

1 Street entrance
2 Stair to attic
3 Attic room
4 Living space
5 Kitchen
6 Rear porch

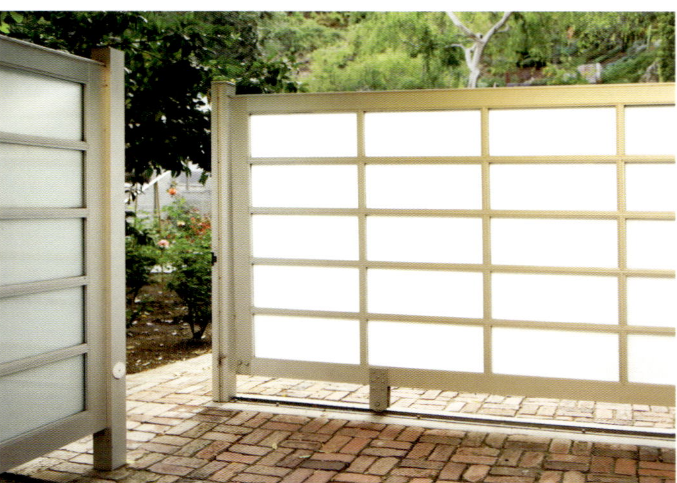

1

2

3

Family|ties

Los Angeles, California, USA
Designed Real Estate

Colour
Most of the colour for the home reflects the materials' natural hues: black and white oak wood, green granite, bricks, cement and stainless steel. These neutral tones – along with white – create a backdrop to the family's furniture, art and collections.

Materials
Granite countertops, limestone flooring and Italian black oak veneered cabinetry give the kitchen a sophisticated look. The same black oak veneered panels and cabinets also appear in the dining room.

The master bedroom features white oak flooring and clean-lined black oak wardrobes, drawer units and storage units. Suspended bronze anodised aluminium shelves next to the bed serve as asymmetrical bedside tables. The master bathroom features granite, limestone and the black oak veneer used elsewhere throughout the house.

Light/Ventilation
LED lights are used to dramatic effect at the terraced steps to the house entrance. At night, fibre optic lights in the pool and spa illuminate the bodies of water in varying hues. Kazovsky designed the inverted L-shaped light fixtures that define the edges of the garden and dining area.

Advice
Listen to what the house tells you. Look at the existing situation, and really take advantage of what is already there. Keep what's great and change what isn't. Be open and flexible to what may occur during the renovation – you might find delightful surprises that add character and interest.

4

This house is sited close to Hollywood's bustling streets, but is visually and aurally isolated from the clamour and activity associated with big city life. Architect Alla Kazovsky wanted a family home that would maximise the potential of the site; she also wanted to involve her children in the design. Most of the artwork showcased throughout the house is by Kazovksy's daughters and the children selected the light fixtures and colour themes in their rooms. ■ The house is entered through the living room, where the existing vaulted wood-beam ceiling and brick walls were retained and new quarter-sawn white oak flooring was installed. A new glass-and-wood entry door ushers light liberally into the room. Brick wall openings into and out of the living room are outlined in steel. ■ The new dining room was created by reducing the kitchen's original size and breaking down a wall to open the space. New stainless-steel appliances, granite countertops, limestone flooring, track lighting and Italian black oak veneered cabinetry give the kitchen a sophisticated look. Black oak veneered panels were added to the perimeter of the cabinets over the sink, lower cabinets and some appliances to create the appearance of free-standing furniture. Instead of a splashback behind the sink, a long window looks onto the redesigned and expanded patio outside. ■ In the dining room, black oak veneered panels and cabinets are suspended over the floor, virtually floating above the quarter sawn white oak flooring that continues from the living room. Removing the existing kitchen wall and all of its associated electrical wiring to create this expanded space led to the innovative solution of constructing a small holding wall to contain the wiring. It doubles as a provocative, shelved niche space. Expansive sliding glass doors span the dining room and part of the family room, opening onto the patio. ■ The charms of the existing house linger in the vaulted wood-beam ceiling of the master bedroom. Kazovsky nearly doubled the size of the existing master bathroom and, in doing so, created a charismatic, uneven ceiling line. The master bedroom's generous windows look on to the deck and pool. ■ The north wing of the house comprises the kids' wing – two bedrooms with beds, storage units, and accessories designed by Kazovsky, and a full bathroom. A shower, new bathtub and two-basin counter are added to the expanded bathroom. ■ The deck includes custom seating space – made of precast benches that also function as guardrails – a fire pit, and a spa with L-shaped seating oriented towards the fire pit and made of the same tile as the waterline. ■

1 The home is shaded by abundant trees
2 Translucent entry gate allows light flow
3 A garden path leads to the family home
4 Back of the house prior to renovation

1 Porch
2 Living room
3 Bedroom
4 Hallway
5 Bath
6 Bedroom
7 Den
8 Kitchen
9 Bedroom
10 Laundry
11 Pantry
12 Bath
13 Master bedroom

1 Porch
2 Living room
3 Bedroom
4 Bath
5 Bedroom
6 Powder room
7 Family room
8 Dining room
9 Kitchen
10 Laundry
11 Office
12 Bath
13 Master bedroom

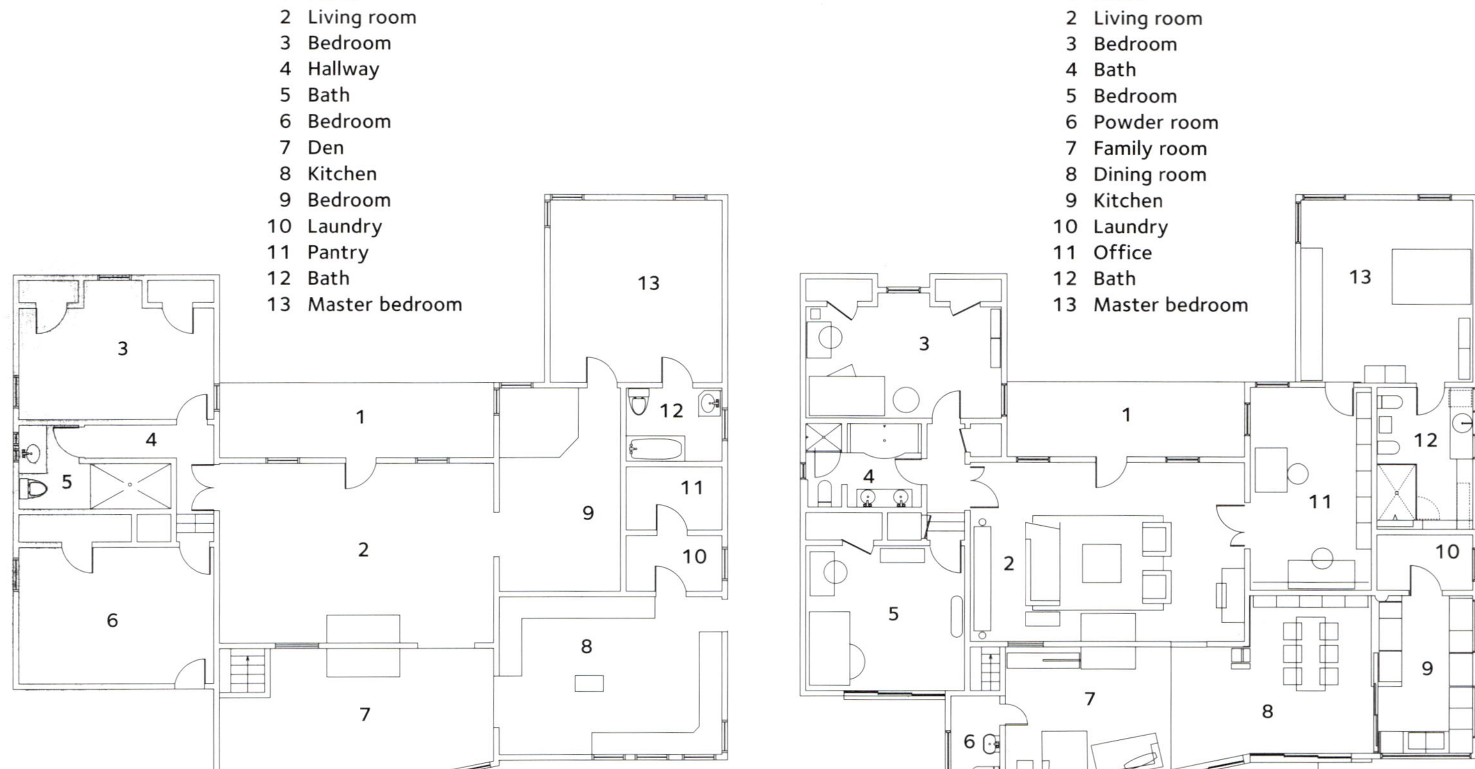

7

8

9

10

11

5 Floor plan before (left); floor plan after (right)

6 Dining room leads seamlessly to kitchen

7 Glass walls open the house to the outdoors

8 Frosted glass doors and interior sidelights keep light flowing

9 Custom touches add delight

10 Dark wood creates sophisticated kitchen

11 Kitchen prior to renovation

12

12 *The architect designed all the beds in the house*

13 *The kids helped decorate their rooms*

14 *Living area prior to renovation*

15 *Pass-through window before is transformed after*

16 *Existing brick and beams were cleaned and maintained*

17 *Living room embraces both modern and rustic sensibilities*

13

14

15

16

17

18

19

20

The Ultimate Urban Makeover

18 *Back patio includes climbing vines on custom light poles*

19 *Water feature mosaic was inspired by the architect's daughter's painting*

20 *New pool has integrated seating and lighting*

21 *Deck overlooks the Hollywood Hills*

Photography by Josh Perrin

1

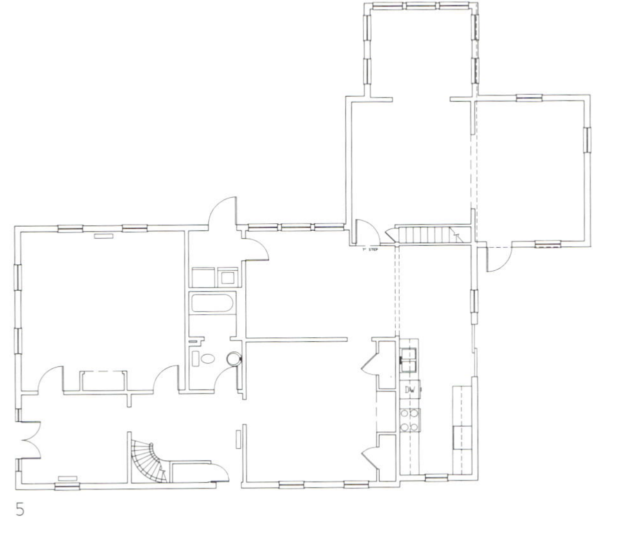

2

3

4

1	Covered porch	13	Family room	18	Nanny's suite
2	Mudroom	14	Existing bedroom	19	Bathroom
3	Two-car garage	15	Existing nursery	20	Closet
4	Existing brick patio	16	Existing bathroom	21	Master bedroom
5	Breakfast area	17	Master bathroom	22	Closet
6	Office			23	Master sitting room
7	Existing dining room				
8	Kitchen				
9	Butler's pantry				
10	Existing stair hall				
11	Existing foyer				
12	Existing sitting room				

5

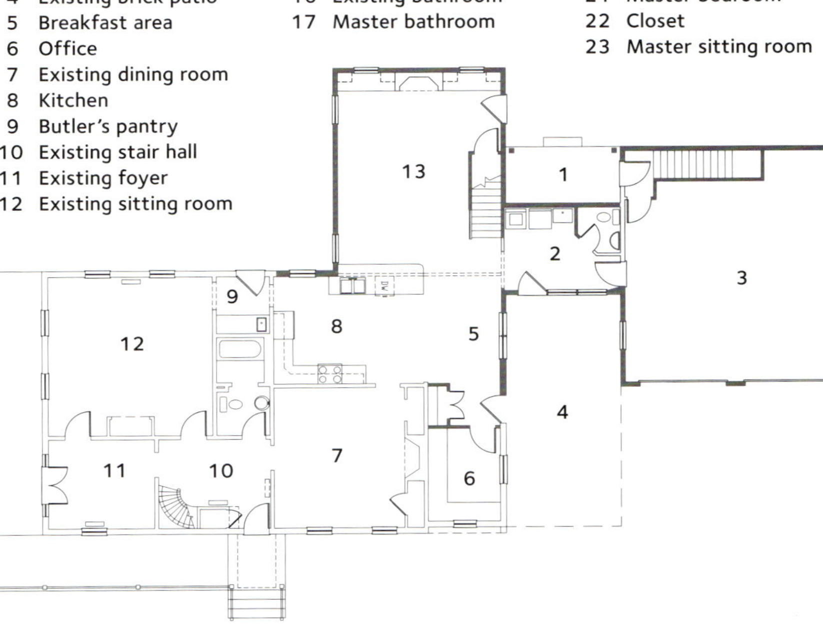

6

Farmhouse|for a|family

Hanover, Maryland, USA
Architecture by Design

LIGHT/VENTILATION

Additional light and ventilation were provided by the renovations to the house. Especially significant was the area that once housed the kitchen and gave way to a more practical use. The new two-storey addition provided essential light and ventilation, and at the same time, improved access and circulation within.

COLOUR

The colours used in this home were of the traditional palette. The exterior is white with black shutters. Inside, the new spaces feature a warm chocolate and crème colour combination that accents the large ceramic tiles within the kitchen area and the Berber carpet in the family space. The new master bedroom space had a 14-foot-high tray ceiling that allowed the adventurous use of a medium slate-blue wall and a bright white ceiling, thus accentuating the ceiling and height of the space.

ADVICE

Old houses can be plagued with mould, sagging ceilings, inefficient plumbing and rising damp. These detractions must be addressed by experts. Be adventurous when it comes down to merging, removing or adding spaces. Don't hesitate to convert an established space such as a kitchen into a space with a radically different use, such as a study or a bedroom.

This two-storey farmhouse was built around 1865. Throughout its existence it has had multiple owners and several additions and many problems typical of old homes were in evidence, including mould, sagging ceilings and many compartmentalised spaces. The owners' desire was for a home with a 21st-century feel with modern, extensive open spaces and large sleeping quarters. ■ An existing addition, originally the maids' quarters, was connected via a small, single-storey room. There was no real connection between the space of the second floor of the main house and the second floor of the connected outbuilding. Also, the existing second floor needed more space for this growing family. It was decided to demolish the addition to the main house and rebuild a new and improved addition that links the second level of the existing building with the new and provides space for a much-needed master suite and bath. ■ The main level of this addition would also provide for the expansion and relocation of the kitchen, a home office and a new open space for the family room. Massing was as important to the design as flow and careful attention was spent on providing an addition that would complement the existing without overwhelming it. The front façade was enhanced with a small breezeway housing the laundry facilities and a powder room that links to the garage, which could also be a future home office or guest suite. Space has been provided for in the design of the attic over the garage. The home now provides everything this growing family would need for many years to come. ■

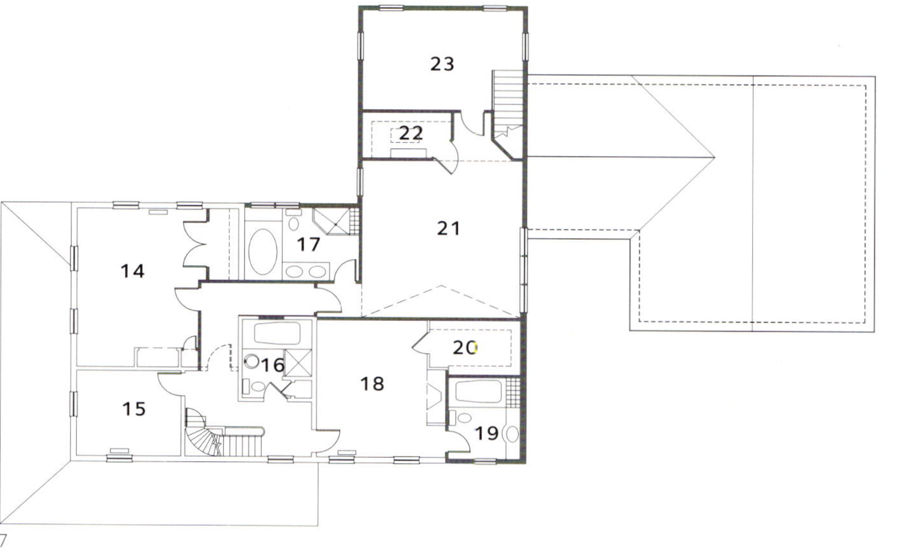

1   The new family room allows much light and ventilation into the new kitchen and informal eating area; the open floor plan is perfect for an active family

2   The front façade was enhanced with a breezeway and garage

3   The existing rear had disconnected elements; now, a proportionate rear façade appears to have always been present

4   The once-small kitchen area now serves as a home office area

5   Floor plan before

6   Ground floor plan after

7   First floor plan after

Photography by Charles Pruett

1   *The portico is formed from brass frames*
Following pages
  Sculptural form of new wing

1

Framed|in|bronze

London, UK
Alison Brooks Architects

COLOUR

Patination of the brass to a grey blue/green shade was achieved with the use of heat and chemicals. The blue/green hue changes depending on the prevailing weather conditions. The only paint, apart from white, is on the interior columns, which are made of four paired angles with spaces between. These are painted a metallic gunmetal colour, which gives them the appearance of steel.

LIGHT/VENTILATION

A continuous strip of glazing on the roof and wall between the original house and the new wing allows natural light to filter into the home. The extension also features bi-fold doors near the kitchen and large glass sliding doors to the dining area. A set of French doors from the living room to the garden at the side of the house also increases the ventilation.

FURNITURE

The clients selected the furniture; the exterior bench, featuring brass cladding, was designed by the architects.

MATERIALS

Bronze was a key material in the design, but other materials help link the interior with the exterior spaces. For example, the rear terrace was paved with the same porcelain tiles that were used in the extension.

ADVICE

Have faith in your architect's ideas. Try not to compromise in the design. It's better to execute one or two ideas well. Too many ideas and materials can become too complicated, both visually to absorb and practically to build.

This townhouse is located on one of South London's major thoroughfares. Surrounded by large and imposing semi-detached homes, it has a typical Victorian layout: left-hand entry, stairs directly ahead, with formal living and dining rooms to the right. Typical of most houses of this period, the service area was at the back, turned away from the garden. ■ The conversion opens up the attic spaces to create lofty children's bedrooms and a kitchen and side extension on the ground floor. The formal dining room at the front of the house, together with the bedrooms on the middle floor, were retained. "Our clients had a huge antique dining table they inherited, so they wanted to retain the formal front dining room. We opened up this room to the front hall with large double doors," says architect Alison Brooks. ■ Originally the owners anticipated a traditional extension but approached the architects with an open mind. "Our brief was to design a kitchen and family/dining room that would be linked to the garden. They were interested in doing something in bronze as they loved the bronze window frames on the newly renovated Dulwich Picture Gallery," says Brooks. While heritage restrictions and privacy concerns limited the rear extension to one level, its sculptural form makes its presence felt from the windows of the upstairs bedrooms. ■ The new wing is treated as a kind of pavilion in the garden. To achieve this, a 1.2-metre-wide strip of glass was inserted between the existing house and the new wing. "The new wing was intended to more or less disappear into the garden. We didn't want to compete with the existing architecture," says Brooks, describing the concept of transparency and working with a single plane, the latter making very precise cuts and folds to create walls, porticos, columns, benches and sunshields. The brass wall panels are used on both the interior and exterior of the new wing. ■ The new extension, which includes the kitchen and family room, is weightless. "It also allows you to feel like you are in the garden even when you're inside. This is partially due to some of the columns being inside and others being outside," says Brooks, who sees the use of metal as being one of the main reasons for the project's success. "It's a very pure expression of a single idea. Working with metal allows a great degree of precision. It's like creating origami," she adds. ■

3

1 Formal dining
2 Study
3 Living room
4 Kitchen
5 WC
6 Dining
7 Deck

4

3 The extension sits lightly next to the Victorian house

4 Floor plan

5 Family dining room is 'in the garden'

6 Patinated brass changes colour with the weather

7 Corner windows slide away to create continuity of space below brass canopy

The Ultimate Urban Makeover

5

6

7

Photography by Dennis Gilbert

1

1 Existing family room
2 Game area
3 Existing utility
4 Billiard room
5 Storage/workshop
6 Pool changing
7 Loggia
8 Kitchen
9 Informal meals
10 Office
11 Laundry/mud room
12 Guest suite
13 Three-car garage
14 Existing den
15 Existing foyer
16 Existing living room
17 Existing bedroom
18 Master suite
19 Master bathroom
20 Studio

2

3

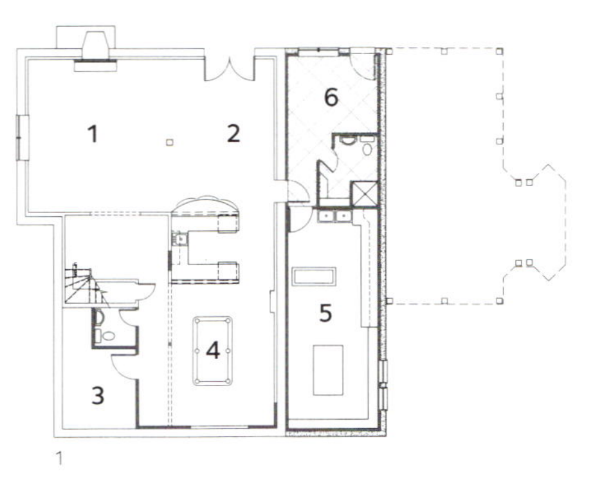

4

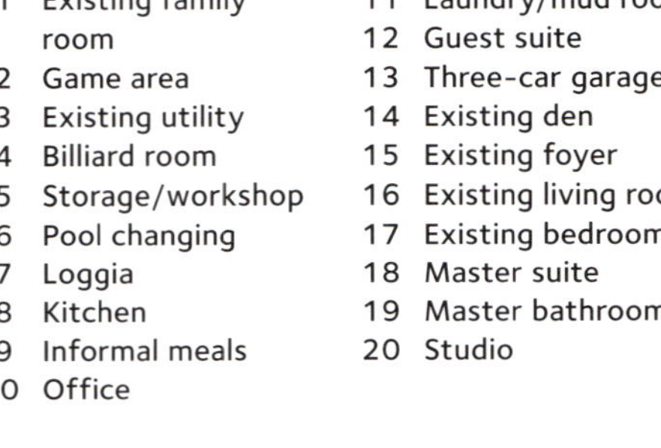

5

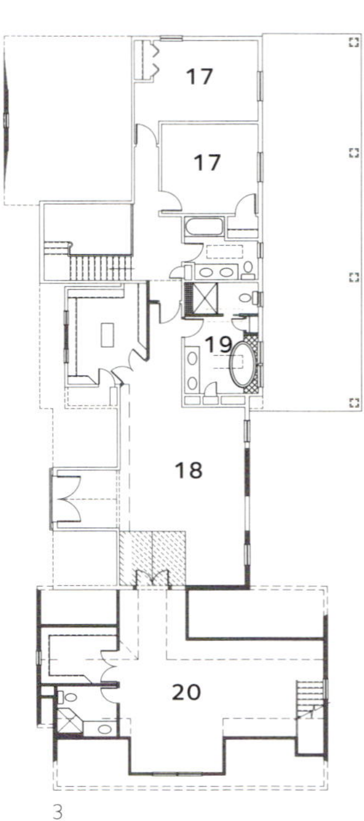

6

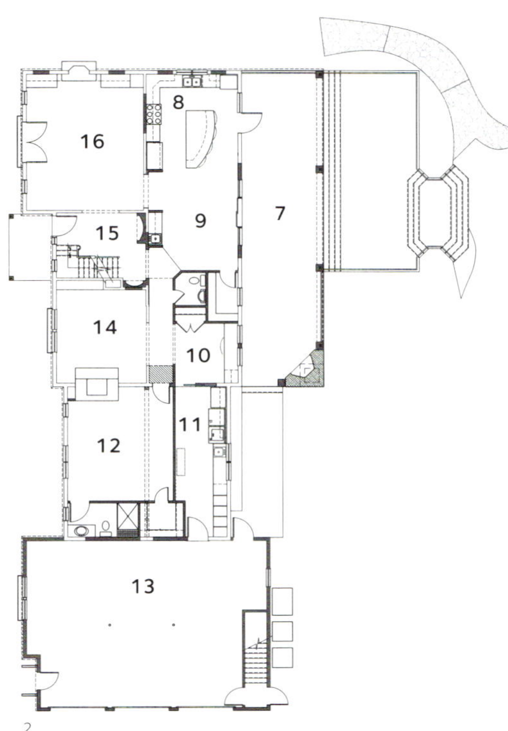

7

French|country-style|elegance

Highland, Maryland, USA
Architecture by Design

This home was purchased by a family that had recently built a large custom home but found its spaces to be too overwhelming and impersonal. They set out to renovate the home by updating and opening up spaces so that they welcome rather than overwhelm. ■ The interior of the house was gutted and a large extension was built to the right side and rear. The aim of the project was to create cohesive, flowing spaces that were also useable and efficient. ■ The separate dining area was combined with the previously small and compartmentalised kitchen breakfast area, forming a large, open space. The existing living room provided a vaulted space with exposed trusses and was altered only by the use of appropriately scaled windows and openings, which replaced the previous overly large windows and tiny side windows. The existing garage space was converted into a warm and welcoming guest suite complete with private bath and walk-in closet. ■ The existing beams on the first floor were partially exposed. During the demolition it was discovered that the underside of the flooring above was of such good quality that it was left fully exposed. ■ On the second floor, the obtrusive master bedroom ceiling was raised to provide appropriate scale and dimension for a master suite. This left an area that was easier to furnish and live in. A large Jacuzzi that previously overwhelmed the master bathroom was replaced with a claw-foot tub, vanities and tables. ■ A loggia was added across the rear to engage the indoor and outdoors. Stone, smooth finish materials and exposed beams make this space warm and welcoming. A pool changing area along with a full bath and small waiting space is beneath the loggia. A new three-car garage with a separate studio space above was constructed on the right side of the house. ■ The addition fits the mass and resembles the original house design so well that it is difficult to detect that it was not part of the original house design. Overall, this project provided the necessary means to impress and entertain as well as provide the creature comforts the owners desired from their home. ■

LIGHT/VENTILATION

The new kitchen/breakfast space replaces the existing compartmentalised area, which is now one large open space suitable for family activities and entertaining. The renovated living room space is in essence unchanged but the scale of the windows has been brought into proportion; the small side windows flanking the fireplace were removed. The paired windows in the guest suite were previously part of the garage. An additional window was added at the front to balance the façade.

COLOUR

The existing colour scheme of warm earth tones was preserved. The additional stone was chosen to accentuate the warm grey siding and new white trim and brackets. The interior colour palette is warm and inviting. The vaulted area in the living space has a dramatic contrast of light-coloured trusses and trim directly adjacent to the ochre ceiling and cayenne walls and provides a dramatic impact upon entry. The sleeping quarters feature light warm tones of green and cream, which tie into the entire house scheme.

ADVICE

To undertake a whole house renovation on this scale, you must be prepared for the time and patience it requires, not to mention the funds required to finance it. If those items don't frighten you then considering a whole house renovation may be the perfect fit for you. With land at a premium in the area where this project is located, this option made the most sense. The base house had merit and was worth salvaging – the benefits far outweighed the trouble.

1 *Basement floor plan after*
2 *Ground floor plan after*
3 *First floor plan after*
4 *Front façade after renovation*
5 *Combining the existing formal dining and kitchen areas allows a much more open and inviting space*
6 *Raising the ceiling in the master bedroom provides a more cohesive and inviting retreat*
7 *The new loggia is a smooth transition from inside to out; a warm stone fireplace provides a focal point without obstructing views of the pool area*

1

2

3

A|fresh|focus

Collingwood, Victoria, Australia
Multiplicity

CIRCULATION

The front door was relocated to the side of the house and the kitchen was relocated from the rear to the centre of the ground floor. The owners now enter into the heart of the house, the kitchen. The original turned-timber staircase leading to the first floor was removed and new timber treads were installed, inserted in the opposite direction to the original staircase. "The original staircase didn't conform to current standards. The treads were too short and the staircase was leaning dangerously to one side," says O'Sullivan.

LIGHT/VENTILATION

Original windows at ground level faced directly onto the side footpath. The dilapidated windows also allowed views directly into the house. To resolve this problem, they were replaced with sashless double-hung glazed windows with translucent glass on the lower half. Interior walls were also removed, with the exception of structural walls. Doors that disappear into cavity walls open up spaces, as does a double-height void above the entrance.

MATERIALS

The clients' brief included the use of tactile materials. To meet this request, recycled timber was used for floors and water-stained elm timber veneer as accent materials for the kitchen cupboards. Concrete also features in bench tops in the kitchen and as the vanity unit in the ensuite. Translucent glass is used in cupboards and screens. "Some materials reflect the light, others tend to absorb it. It's a matter of finding a balance," says O'Sullivan.

COLOURS

While the renovation includes a muted palette of colours such as browns, mochas and aubergines, highlight colours are used in the sliding doors/walls, including 'rocket red', a Chinese lacquered red and 'date palm', a vibrant green.

ADVICE

When renovating a terrace, you are often working with the later additions that have been made to the home, whether from the 1950s, 1980s or later. It's not about stripping things out and starting from scratch. The design should evolve and incorporate appropriate features from the past.

This two-storey terrace, like its neighbours, faces the street. A shotgun corridor to one side of the house originally provided the main thoroughfare. And like many terraces of its time, rooms simply led off the main corridor, starting with the formal rooms at the front. The structure of the original home was as tenuous as the layout. "The area was previously a swamp. The foundations were built on reactive clay. We had to underpin the house by 1.8 metres," says architect Tim O'Sullivan, who worked with partner interior designer Sioux Clark on the renovation of this building. ■ Because the house was located on a corner site, one of the first changes made was to relocate the front door to the side street. The repositioning of the original entrance not only freed up the shotgun corridor running the length of the house, but also allowed the owners direct access to the open-plan kitchen at the heart of the house. ■ The focus of the kitchen is a generous 3-metre-long concrete bench. The kitchen features translucent glass-enclosed shelves and water elm cupboards. A scullery includes a generous stainless steel bench for more serious cooking. "Our clients wanted the design to capture how they live now. The kitchen was pivotal in the design. They like to cook at the same time," says Clark. ■ While a 1980's addition to the home was retained in the renovation, a new edge was created to the living space. A floating ceiling over the living area conceals a pitched roof. To keep within budget constraints, existing doors to a small rear courtyard were also refashioned rather than replaced. ■ The second level includes a reading room/guest bedroom, a powder room that overlooks a void in the entrance, a bathroom/ensuite and the main bedroom. "We didn't see the point of creating a permanently enclosed space for a second bedroom. Our clients might only occasionally have guests to stay," says Clark, who demonstrates how two large floor-to-ceiling sliding doors enclose the space. ■

1   *Light filters through an acrylic and timber screen to the main bathroom*

2   *This former corner pub in its original condition; entry to residence is at far right*

3   *Extent of demolition at ground floor showing new, full-height openings between rooms*

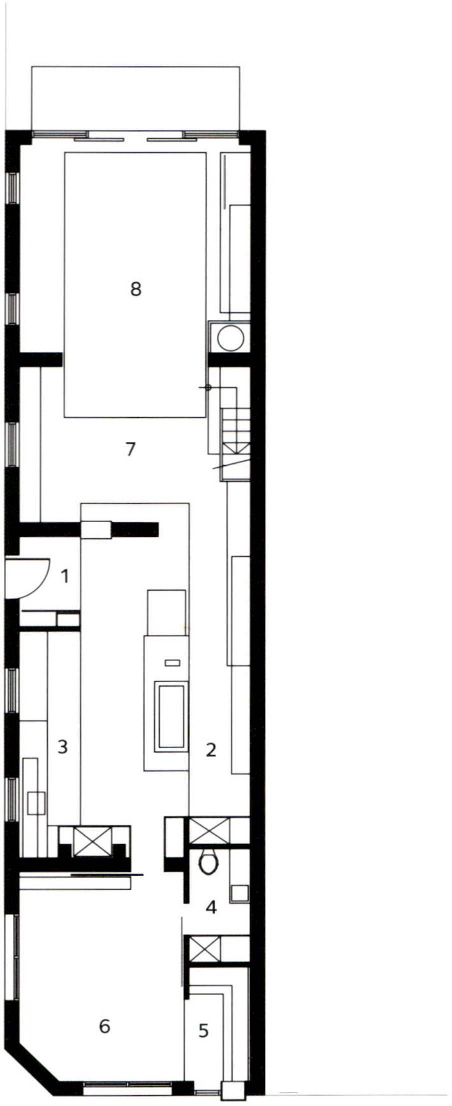

4

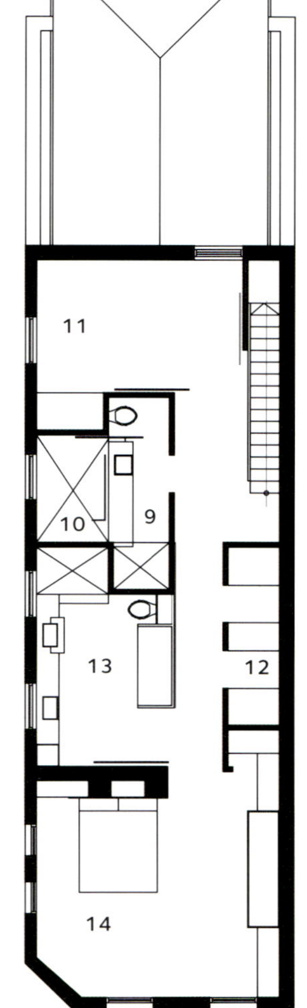

1 Entry
2 Kitchen
3 Scullery
4 Powder room/laundry
5 Music room/library
6 Study
7 Dining
8 Living
9 Ensuite
10 Void
11 Guest bedroom
12 Walk in robe
13 Bathroom
14 Main bedroom

0   4m

5

6

The Ultimate Urban Makeover

7

4 *Ground floor (left) and first floor plan (right) of renovated house*

5 *New steel-clad front doors provides access directly off the street into the kitchen*

6 *Moody tones of stairwell suit its location in the centre of the house*

7 *New living area within former addition with intersecting ceiling that links structures of different periods*

8

9

10

11

8   *Looking towards rear of the property during renovation*

9   *Muted tones and rich texture of kitchen are uplifted by accent colours of full-height sliding door/s*

10   *The transformation of the kitchen space looking towards rear garden*

11   *The upper level, including the main bedroom, is designed with spaces that can open or close to accommodate guests*

12   *Vanity basins in main bathroom are at different heights to accommodate individual requirements*

Photography by Shania Shegedyn

12

The Ultimate Urban Makeover

The|glow of|sandstone

Balmain, New South Wales, Australia
Robert Simeoni Pty Ltd Architects

Colour
The main colour in the house comes from the sandstone walls that appear on both levels. Where the walls are plastered, they often feature large colourful paintings by artists including John Olsen.

Light/Ventilation
Large floor-to-ceiling doors and windows appear at both the front and rear of the house. At the rear, glass doors fold back on themselves to increase natural light. Light, although artificial, also appears on the sandstone walls by means of recessed lighting concealed in the ceiling.

Materials
The materials used in the renovation include stainless steel, timber and polished concrete. Some of the materials in the original home were also lightened. The floorboards in the living and dining areas were limed.

Ventilation
Louvred glass windows feature in the third bedroom upstairs (located in the side wing). Large glass windows and doors at both ends of the house improve ventilation. Large windows above the bath on the ground floor create a sense of bathing outdoors.

Furniture
With two small children, the owners steered away from precious furniture, preferring hardy contemporary designs made of leather. Furniture was kept to a minimum in keeping with the scale of the house.

Advice
Have patience when you are renovating this style of home. People now want to live in light-filled spaces that are quite transparent. But this is fighting against the typology of these homes. You need to examine all the options.

Built in the 1850s, this two-storey sandstone house has been drawn into the 21st century. Originally, a ship builder's home, the house is now occupied by a couple with two young children. Its prized location, overlooking Sydney Harbour, more than compensates for its relatively modest size (approximately 100 square metres). ■ Recently redesigned by architect Robert Simeoni, the house includes four original rooms: two upstairs bedrooms with living and dining rooms downstairs. While the upstairs bedrooms were restored, the two rooms on the ground floor were reworked. The wall surrounding the fireplace in the living room was removed. "I wanted to open up the ground floor and strengthen the connection to the rear garden," says Simeoni. ■ An elongated wing that had been added to the house in the 1940s was gutted. "The kitchen was dark and quite oppressive. It had just been tacked on to the house without much thought," says Simeoni. With a new galley-style kitchen at one end and a bathroom at the other, this wing now benefits from large glass windows and doors at each end. The new kitchen features stainless steel bench tops, sycamore timber cupboards and polished concrete flooring. "I tried to use materials that displayed the same degree of strength as materials used in the original home," says Simeoni. ■ One of the pleasures of renovating the house came with the removal of the plaster concealing the original sandstone walls. "There's a wonderful glow in the house when the sunlight reflects off the walls," says Simeoni. A display module links the side wing to the house. Made of MDF, the unit features cutout shelving the same dimensions as the sandstone bricks. "It's a linking device. But it partially conceals the new staircase. I didn't want to create a sharp division between the old and new," says Simeoni. ■

1 *Inside dining and living spaces open to new private courtyard with folding doors that wrap around wall and 'liberate' the corner*
2 *New display contains the laundry pod and provides a new focus to the dining room and a link to the kitchen*
3 *View to new courtyard raised to align with interior floor level*

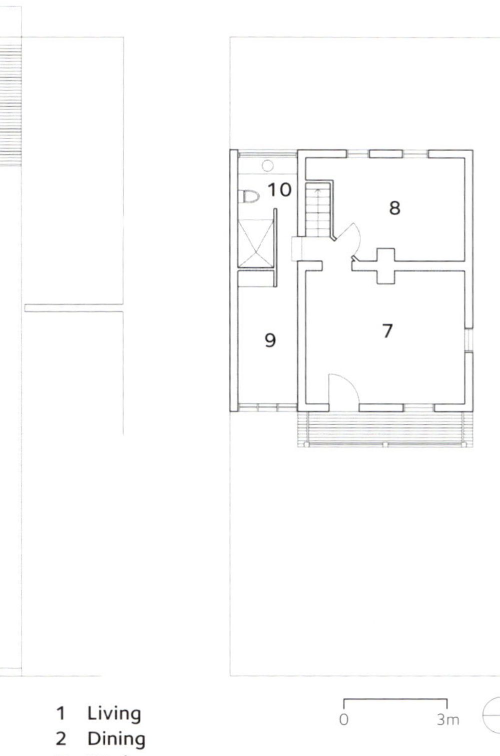

1 Living
2 Dining
3 Kitchen
4 Bathroom
5 Courtyard
6 Front terrace
7 Bedroom
8 Bedroom
9 Study
10 Bathroom

0   3m

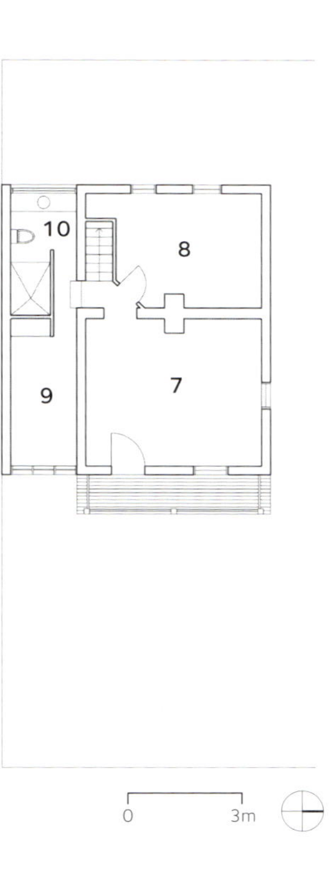

4   Ground floor plan (left); first floor plan (right)
5   New louvre window inserts to front terrace
6   Detail of new timber folding doors and liberated corner wall
7   Light from ceiling cutouts imparts glow to sandstone wall
8   New kitchen with view through to bathroom and pond beyond
9   New laundry pod/display unit acts as link with new kitchen/bathroom
10   New bathroom arrangement with multifunction sliding door divides wall storage unit
11   Bathroom opens up with folding windows to adjacent pond

Photography by Robert Simeoni and Aaron Pocock

The Ultimate Urban Makeover

9

10

11

Greenwich|Village|townhouse

Greenwich Village, New York, USA
Hariri & Hariri – Architecture

COLOUR

While white walls prevail in the interior spaces, they are animated by the changing light conditions during the day. Colour is integral to the materials used, including polished concrete flooring at ground level and hardwood flooring on the first floor. The indoor/outdoor pond, featuring aquamarine tiles, provides further colour.

LIGHT

Light streams into the home via a double-storey glass curtain wall at the rear. The interior walls take the form of translucent glass, either as fixed or moveable screens. The entire space is kept loft-like and open: the staircase has open treads, a simple steel handrail and a glass balustrade.

FURNITURE

The furniture is a combination of the owner's own products, his collection of old and new artefacts and pieces designed and selected specifically for this space. The fountain, for example, is a piece of carved marble from the Mogul period, part of the owner's collection.

This townhouse is located on the first two floors of a typical brownstone building in Greenwich Village. It was designed as a home, gallery and inspiring work environment for its occupant, a product designer who spends half his time in India. ■ "Our client wanted an environment where art and architecture would intertwine. He also wanted to accommodate and exhibit his old and new artefacts and products. Conceptually this project was developed as a temple for the art, a sanctuary for the soul and a refuge for the body," says architect Gisue Hariri. ■ The classified building features an intact façade. However, the architects were faced with a partially demolished interior at the start of the renovation. The architects gutted all 180 square metres of existing floor space and a 17-square-metre, double-storey extension was added to the rear. As the entire interior has been reworked, there is no distinction between the existing part of the house and the addition. But in contrast to the original brick façade, the rear features a double-storey glass curtain wall. ■ The whole space is organised around light. Entry to the home is on the upper level. Upon arrival, a light-wall greets visitors and signals the centre of the apartment. The light-wall is a vertical connector between the two floors, organising the space and circulation, while providing illumination for both floors. ■ The spaces on both floors are continuous from the street to the garden, allowing natural light to penetrate and filter through. All the wet elements, including the kitchen, shower and powder room, are along the east wall and are concealed behind translucent screens on tracks. These screens create privacy for the spaces behind, while still allowing light in. The dining area is open to a double-storey volume, looking into the garden. A shallow trough of water with a fountain at the end continues into the garden, blurring the interior and exterior spaces. ■ A double-storey sanctuary is one of the important aspects of the renovation. Here space, light, water, fire (an open fireplace in the living area) and earth inspire and highlight the collaboration between architecture and art. ■

2   *This duplex apartment is a home, gallery and inspiring work environment for its occupant*

3   *Light-filled double-storey sanctuary at end opens to terrace and is enclosed by curtain wall*

4   *Stucco sculptural fireplace is main element of living room*

5 *Ground floor plan*

6 *First floor plan*

7 *Along light wall, a metal stair with translucent treads leads to main living room*

8 *All wet elements – kitchen, shower and powder room – are behind sliding translucent screens along the east wall*

9 *Detail of kitchen*

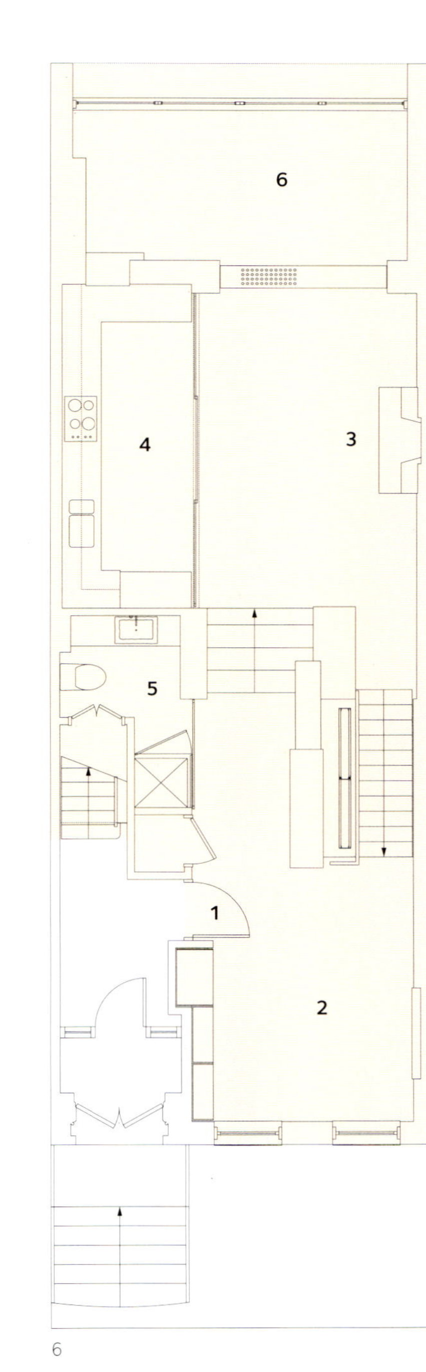

5

0   3.6m

6

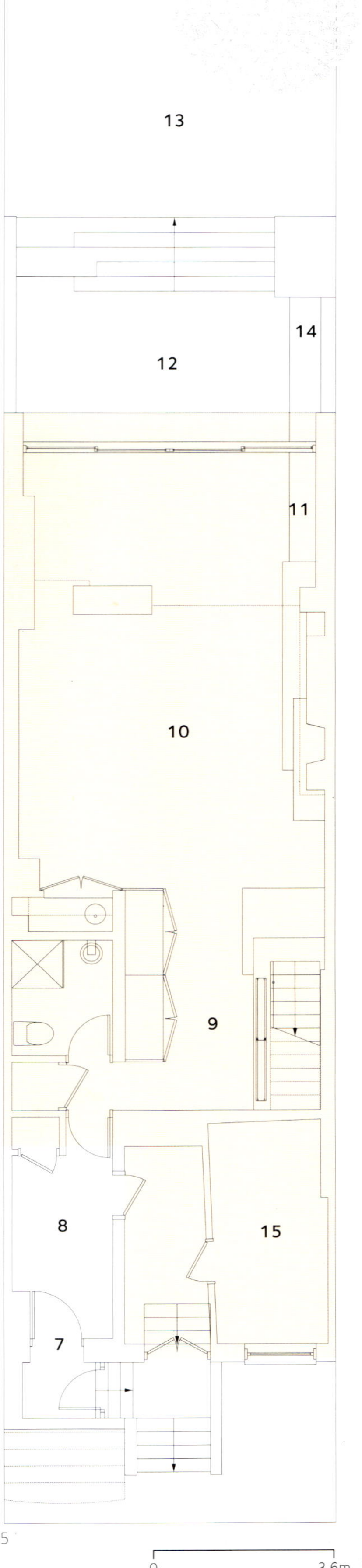

7

1 First floor entry
2 Library/bedroom
3 Dining
4 Kitchen
5 Bathroom
6 Open to below
7 Ground floor entry
8 Foyer
9 Stair hall
10 Living room
11 Water channel
12 Terrace
13 Garden
14 Fountain
15 Mechanical room

The Ultimate Urban Makeover

8

9

Opposite *The light wall greets visitors upon entry*
11 *Bathroom detail*

Photography by Paul Warchol (1,4,7,9–11)
courtesy Hariri & Hariri – Architecture (2,3,8)

11

1   *Street elevation indicating the joining of the two houses*
2   *Linkway between the two houses*
3   *Rear elevation*

Joined|at the|hip

Toorak, Victoria, Australia
Black Kosloff Knott (BKK) Architects

CIRCULATION

The original corridors were incorporated in the design. The light-filled spaces at the rear are visible as soon as you enter either front door. A new piece of joinery in the contemporary wing allows both parents and children to have their own space, while still feeling connected to the larger spaces.

VENTILATION

The entire rear façade was opened up with floor-to-ceiling glass sliding doors. The central light well, with its surrounding windows, also draws out hot air from the house.

MATERIALS

The contemporary addition is painted brick, similar to that used on the original homes. The rear frame/eaves surrounding the two homes are made of messmate, which has weathered to a silvery grey.

COLOUR

The clients' love of the colour green led to the choice of mint green for the laminate kitchen cupboards, for the wall of joinery between the children's play area and the main living areas. Green also appears in the studded rubber flooring in the bathrooms.

FURNITURE

Instead of buying all new furniture, the owners incorporated some of their old pieces such as bentwood chairs. "The children are young. It's important for them to use the house rather than walking around the perimeters," says Knott.

ADVICE

Orientation is critical when planning a renovation. If you have the right amount of sunlight, the rooms are used. This house enjoys a sunny aspect, receiving direct light for most of the day.

This house is an amalgamation of two separate properties. One is a single-fronted Victorian terrace, built in the 1880s; the other is Edwardian, built in the early 19th century. "Our clients owned the Edwardian house. They were thinking of extending it when the adjoining house came on the market," says architect Simon Knott. ■ Both houses required work. The Edwardian house included a late 1970's addition while the Victorian house featured several layers of additions, beginning from the 1950s. "We discussed building a new house on the two sites. But both houses were relatively intact and contributed to the period streetscape," says Knott. "Both houses were well constructed, with high ceilings and decorative embellishments," he adds. ■ The original parts of both houses were converted into bedrooms. The parents' bedroom, ensuite and study are located in the Edwardian home, while the two children's bedrooms and bathroom are located in the Victorian terrace. A spacious contemporary wing at the rear of both houses ties the two properties together. On one side are the kitchen, living and dining areas. On the other side, separated by a wall of cupboards is the children's play area. A large timber deck leading from the living area and the play area further strengthens the relationship between the two houses. A deep verandah/eave, made of messmate, frames the rear of the new wing. "The frame sets up the view into the back garden and defines the new wing," says Knott. ■ To further strengthen the bond between the two houses, the metre-wide gap separating the two was converted into a lightwell as well as a bridge. Windows in both houses open into the lightwell. "The parents can be in the kitchen and still look through to the children's wing. It's passive supervision," says Knott. And unlike some renovations, where the garden continues at the same level as the living spaces, in this instance, the levels change. "You have to walk up, before moving into the garden. The idea was to define the threshold rather than blur the lines," adds Knott. ■

4

5

6

4 Threshold/deck

5 Detail of timber frame

6 Frame is 'clipped onto' existing house

7 Floor plan

8,9 The clients' love of the colour green led to the choice of mint green for the laminate kitchen cupboards and for joinery walls in other parts of the house

Photography by Peter Bennetts
David Mitchener

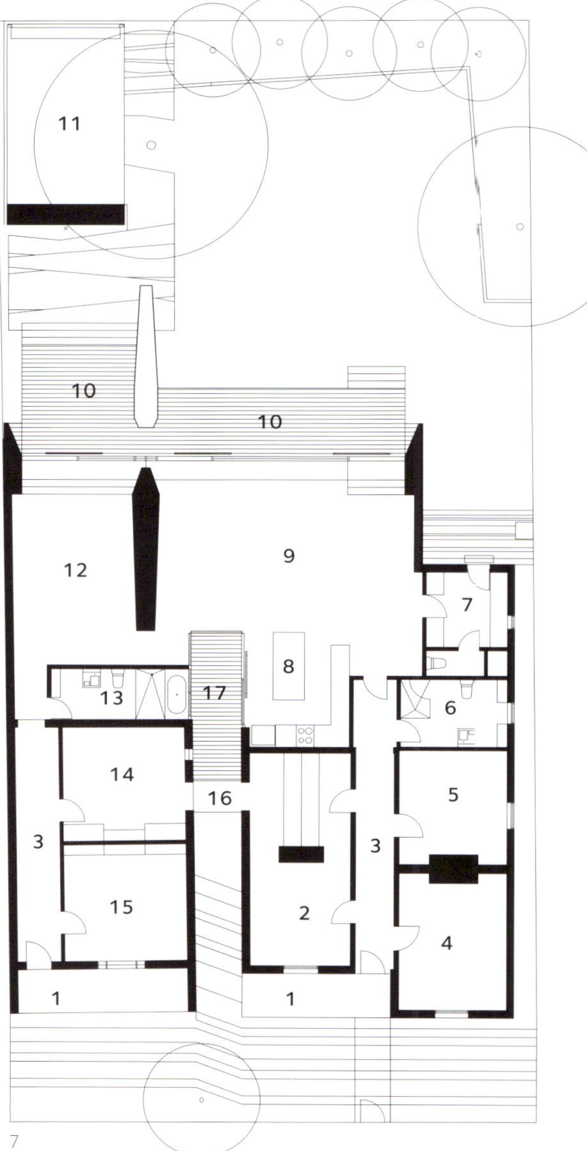

7

8

9

1 Studio
2 Master bedroom
3 Living room
4 Dining room
5 Kitchen
6 Deck
7 Hall
8 Bedroom 1
9 Bedroom 2
10 Living room below

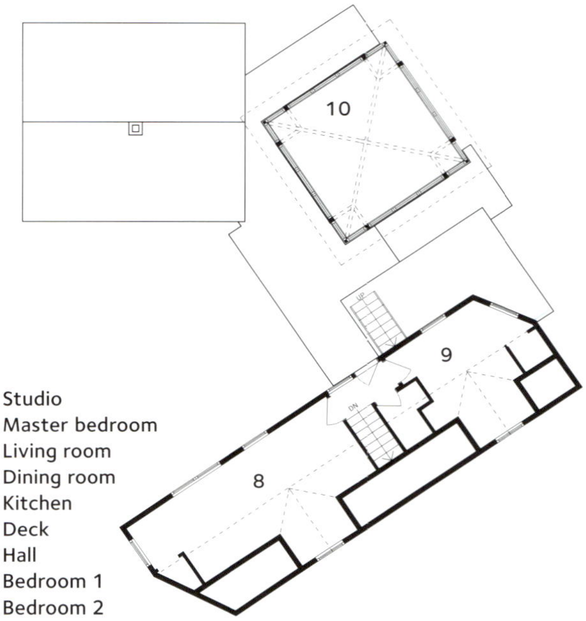

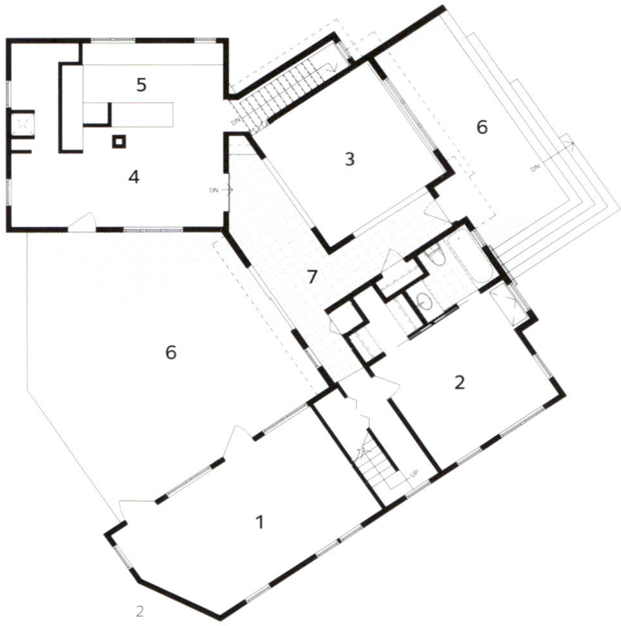

1 Studio
2 Master bedroom
3 Living room
4 Dining room
5 Kitchen
6 Bedroom 1
7 Bedroom 2

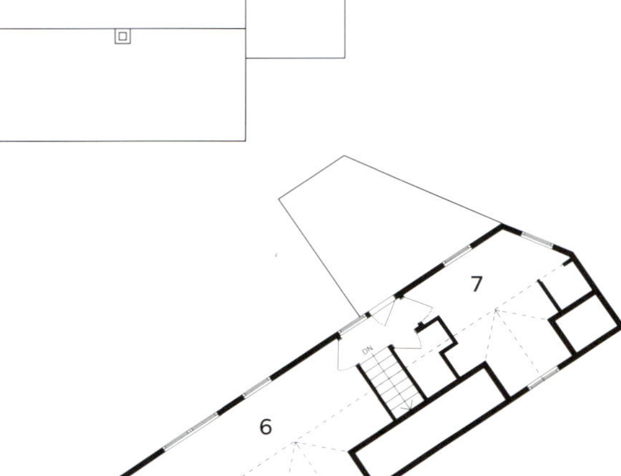

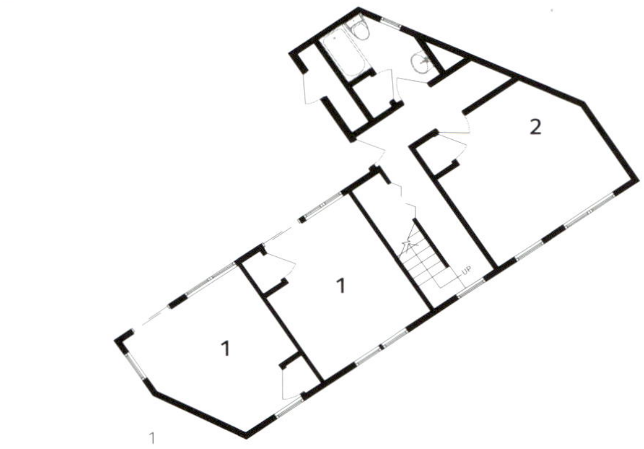

3

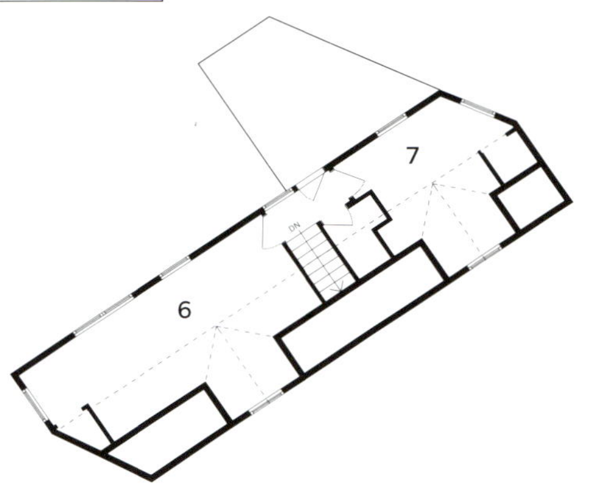

4

The Ultimate Urban Makeover

Wellfleet, Massachusetts, USA
Hammer Architects

LIGHT/VENTILATION

Natural ventilation was a critical design concern as the house is occupied throughout the summer months. To avoid air conditioning and reduce energy consumption, high operable clerestory windows introduce light from all directions and capture the prevailing sea breezes to provide ventilation. These windows are in turn shielded from the weather by an overhanging pyramid roof permitting their continuous use. The large, multi-paned glass window wall visually connects the interior with the garden and the woods beyond. The rear of the house opens on to an enclosed private landscaped courtyard surrounded by the three wings.

COLOUR

The focus of the interior is the ceiling of the living room where the warm-toned, exposed fir-beamed structure echoes the pyramidal-shaped roof. The interior of the home is filled with natural light and the extra-high white walls display the artists' collection of paintings, photographs and wall sculptures. Natural slate and bamboo are the prevailing flooring materials.

ADVICE

Linking two independent structures can often solve the problems associated with heating and cooling. In this case, because a new building linked the two older structures, it also created a basement for additional services and facilities.

As a result its natural beauty and of the extraordinary quality of light, the outer Cape has long been a magnet for artists. Since 1915, when prominent artists such as Charles Hawthorne and Oscar Giebrich began painting and exhibiting the work of other local artists in Provincetown, the end of Cape Cod has become a refuge for artists and was known as 'the biggest art colony in the world'. ■ The original house, owned by a painter and a photographer couple, is located near Wellfleet Harbor. The home is situated on a wooded site and access to a rooftop 'widow's walk' provides lovely water views. The design for the renovations by Hammer Architects began with two existing and completely separate structures. ■ A modified Cape-style house built in the 1970s contained the artist's studios, bedrooms and bathrooms while an adjacent renovated garage accommodated the living room, kitchen and dining room. Because the house was built as a summer retreat, it was unheated, and circulation between the two buildings was problematic in inclement weather. These distinct components were connected and combined in a new, year-round residence by the introduction of a towering central element that contains a new living room, entry hall and master bedroom suite. The cubic form of this central mass, with its large openings, unifies the other disparate forms and creates an overall design with a strong visual focus. ■

6

5

1   Ground floor plan before (bottom); first floor plan before (top)
2   Ground floor plan after (bottom); first floor plan after (top)
3   Rear courtyard with connecting addition and pyramidal roof
4   Interior view of living room ceiling with exposed structure
5   View of new street façade with central entry
6   View of living room with monumental window

Photography by Mark D. Hammer, Hammer Architects

1

2

3

4

Moving|on from the|past

Hawthorn, Victoria, Australia
O'Connor + Houle Architecture

LIGHT

Floor-to-ceiling windows/doors frame the new wing, increasing the amount of light entering the home. Additional light was drawn into the new space from celestial windows concealed in the new roofline. The new wing was set back 1.2 metres from the original home, to allow light to enter from all sides of the new wing. The study area features generous glazing, extending 4.5 metres, to catch the morning light.

COLOUR

Several connections between the old and new were formed. For example, Baltic pine floorboards in the original section of the house were stained black. Concrete floors in the new wing were also treated with a black pigment. The front period rooms feature bright polychromatic colours that lift the weight of the original masonry. In contrast, the new work appears in greys, whites and monochromes. "Balance is important, whether it's the use of colour or the choice of materials," says O'Connor.

MANIPULATING ORIGINAL ROOMS

O'Connor describes Victorian rooms as 'stubborn'. "It's about overcoming the gravity of the old building," says O'Connor, referring to the load-bearing masonry. "These buildings don't offer flexibility," he adds. Many of the rooms, for example, are too large for one use and not quite large enough to create two uses. However, the one of the bedrooms was successfully segmented to create an ensuite, a walk-in dressing area and a separate laundry and powder room. A glass screen was used to define the separate functions.

ADVICE

Combining the old with the new is rarely black and white. "It's about creating linkages between the two styles. But clear divisions, where the new starts and the old finishes, are also important. Both periods are strengthened and enriched in the process," says O'Connor.

This Hawthorn brick terrace was in a precarious state. A side wall displayed a large and expanding crack. "We had to carefully stitch it back together using stainless steel rods," says architect Stephen O'Connor. Fortunately, the interiors were relatively intact, complete with fireplaces, cornices and wide skirting boards. ■ The terrace had been added to in the 1980s. The irregularly shaped addition, which included a kitchen and living area, also featured a separate 'spa room', centred in the space. "It was a fairly unusual arrangement. It wasn't going to work for our clients," says O'Connor, who completely removed the 1980's additions. "Our clients wanted a contemporary renovation. But they wanted the new work to relate to the terrace as well as the garden," he adds. ■ The original home was restored, with the formal living area now acting as a parents' retreat. Three of the four bedrooms were retained in the design; the fourth bedroom was transformed into an ensuite and walk-in dressing area. There was also sufficient space for a laundry and powder room. ■ A completely new wing was added to the home, via what the architects refer to as a 'link'. The link, which takes the form of a concrete rendered box, separates the old from the new. It forms a 1.2-metre-long bridge between the Victorian terrace and the new glazed wing. "We wanted to be able to bring additional light into the home, even though the original home is oriented in the other direction," says O'Connor. ■ The new wing comprises a lounge at one end of the space, featuring an open fireplace. At the other end is the kitchen, which conceals a study behind. A door, which appears to be a pantry door in the kitchen, is actually the door to the study. The architects were also keen to create a strong axis point from the front door to the rear yard to strengthen the relationship between the two styles. A cluster of birch trees outside a rear door is aligned with the front door. The architects used a heavy timber frame surrounding the glazed door to the rear garden. ■

1   1970's additions prior to demolition
2   1970's addition removed
3   Detail of structural cracking to original fabric
4   Rear of house showing new additions

5

6

5 Living/dining area overlooks back garden and lap pool
6 Victorian sitting room with art works by Melinda Harper and Clement Meadmore
7 Dining/living area
8 Titanium zinc 'link' acts as threshold between old and new parts of house

7

8

1 Front yard
2 Verandah
3 Bedroom 1
4 Dressing
5 Bath 1
6 Laundry
7 Bath 2
8 Courtyard
9 Living
10 Dining
11 Garage
12 Lawn
13 Kitchen
14 Lounge
15 Dining
16 Bedroom 2
17 Study
18 Pool

0　　　　5m

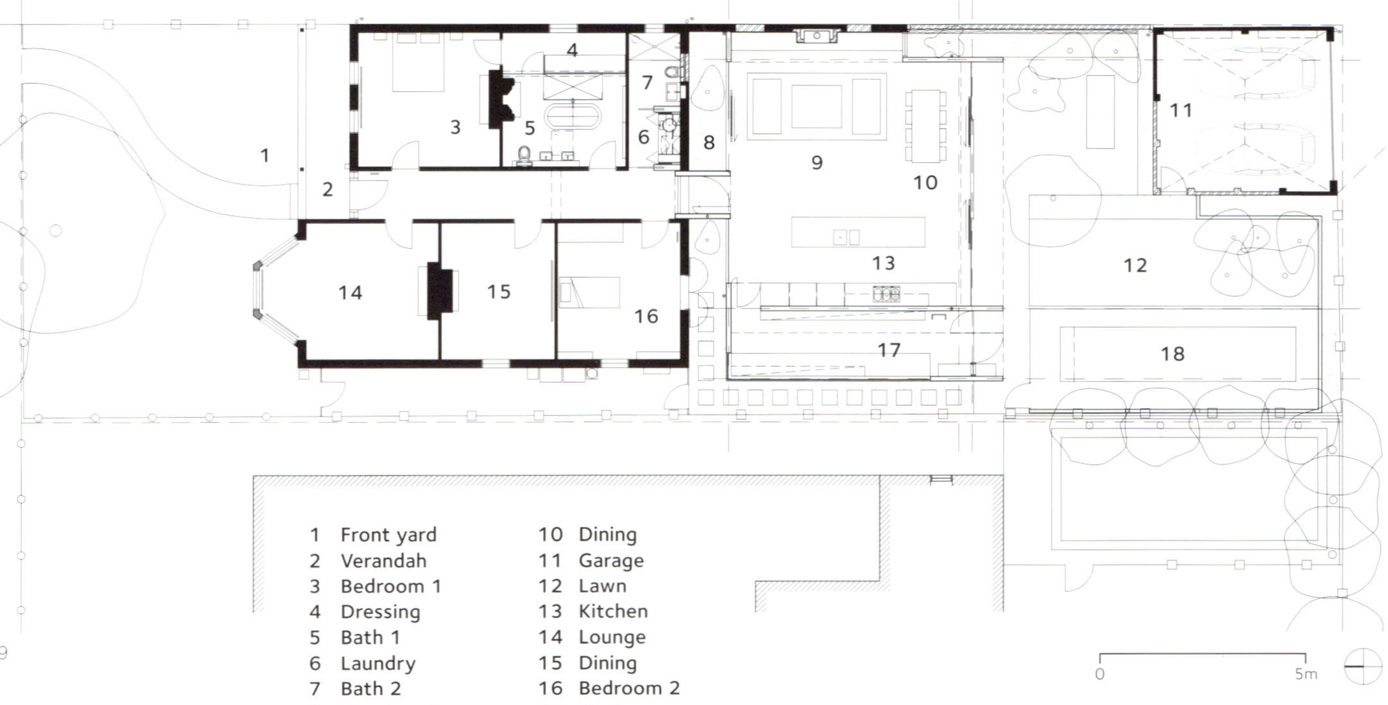

11

9 *Floor plan*
10 *Kitchen with concealed door to study*
11 *Study with large pivot door opening out to pool area*

12

13

14

12 *Victorian master bedroom*

13 *Master ensuite*

14 *Children's bedroom with custom-made
'bubbles' joinery*

Photography by Shannon Pawsey

1 Carefully restored, the street elevation has changed little since the house was built in 1732
2 The house forms part of an intact Georgian terrace in London's Soho
3 A stainless steel bridge spans the enlarged lightwell, formed from the original coal chute
4 Limewashed brickwork in the basement gym and illuminated external vault beyond
5 View to the courtyard garden from the restored staircase

1

2

3

4

5

A|new way of|living

Soho, London, UK
Form Design Architecture

Colour

Apart from the main bedroom and ensuite, which are painted white, most of the other rooms in the house are painted in a stone colour, more appropriate to the original panelling. "We didn't want the house to feel dark. The blue lacquered joinery in the kitchen also adds a certain lightness," says Neale.

Light/Ventilation

The basement vault was opened up to let more light in. This was limewashed and up-lights were installed. At the top floor, new windows and doors that open onto a roof terrace were installed. Muslin blinds appear on many of the windows, allowing light into the rooms, but shielding views from neighbouring homes.

The main bedroom/retreat on the top floor was fitted with air conditioning, new doors and windows. New windows were also added to the basement shower room and a pair of glazed double doors was installed in the basement vault.

Furniture

The furniture is deliberately contemporary. Modern elements such as kitchen units have been treated as furniture. These modular insertions could, if desired, be removed in the future to leave the original fabric intact.

Advice

The terraced house form, from the Georgian era to the present, is very resilient to social change and remains eminently suitable for modern-day living. You may not use the rooms in the same way as the original occupants, but the layout can still work for you.

In 1732, when this row house was built, the kitchen was located in the basement and the workshop was in the garret, directly below the roof. Fast-forward to the 21st century and the configuration has completely changed. The owner's bedroom is in the garret and the basement has been converted into guest accommodation. "The original architect John Meard, as well as the early occupants of the house, would have been shocked by this current arrangement," says architect Mike Neale, who reworked the heritage-listed house. ■ Located in Soho, London, the street was originally lined with Georgian houses, constructed by Meard, Master of the Worshipful Company of Carpenters. Today, only those houses on the south side of the street survive. While Soho is now a fashionable area to live, by the 1970s, the whole area, including this house, had become somewhat rundown and seedy. "Little or no maintenance work had been carried out on the house for some years before we became involved," says Neale. ■ The original features in the house, including the timber panelling, were restored. New plumbing and electrical services were also inserted. Unfortunately, many of the period features, such as brass-rim locks, door handles, shutters and mouldings had been removed. However, there were some surprises in the renovation, including the discovery of original timber wall panelling in a bathroom, behind 1970's plasterboard lining. ■ As the house is classified, all original rooms had to be retained in the renovation. But the kitchen is now located on the ground floor rather than tucked away in the basement. The basement is now a guest suite, with a new shower created from the previous coal cellar. A previously unused storeroom is now a small gym. ■ While the house is spread over five levels, it is relatively compact (approximately 200 square metres). The ground floor comprises the dining area and kitchen, together with a utility room. A living area, study and bathroom are on the first floor and a bedroom, bathroom and dressing area are on the second floor. The main bedroom and ensuite are nestled in the roof space. For the architects, one of the main problems with the renovation was access. "Because the house is located in a narrow pedestrian street, all the materials had to be carried in and out from a small van. Inside the house, the only access up the building was via the relatively tight original staircase," says Neale. ■ The interventions to the house, which include a new stainless steel kitchen with blue

(continued)

lacquered joinery, are clearly contemporary additions. "Power points and light switches posed a particular challenge because some of the original walls lacked depth, making it difficult to conceal wiring," says Neale. The solution to this was to locate many switches in the floor. A stainless steel bridge is also clearly new, providing a link to the small rear garden. The ensuite in the main bedroom is also contemporary, with a raised bath and open shower. ■

7

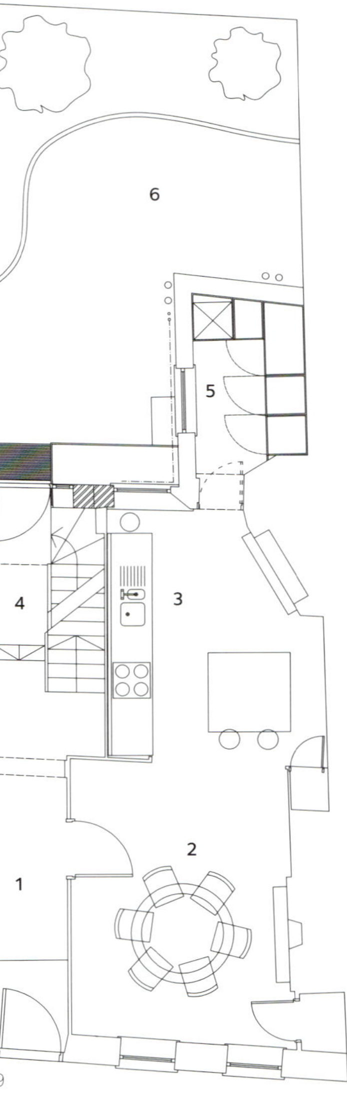

6

8

9

10

13

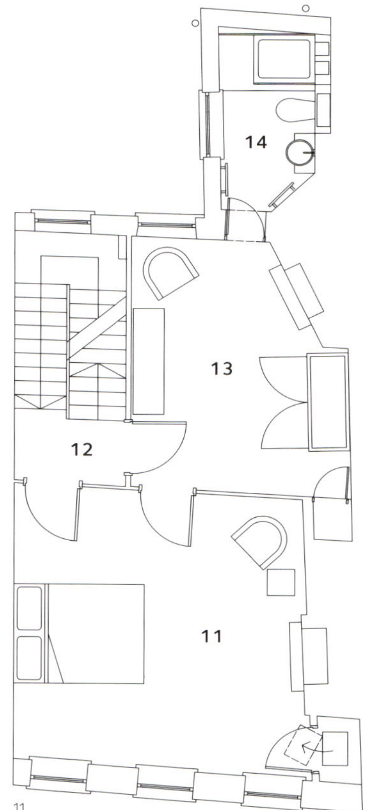

1 Entrance
2 Dining area
3 Kitchen
4 Hall
5 Utility room
6 Garden
7 Living area
8 Landing
9 Study
10 Bathroom
11 Bedroom
12 Landing
13 Dressing room
14 Bathroom
15 Bedroom
16 Landing
17 Bathroom
18 Roof terrace

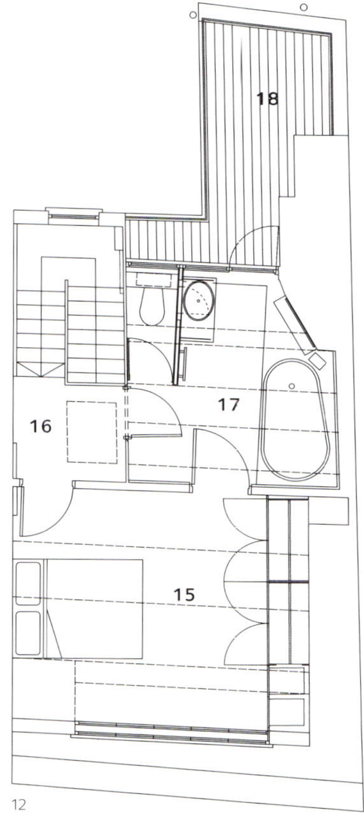

14

11

12

6 *Inserted in the panelled ground floor reception room, the contemporary kitchen has been treated as furniture*

7 *A simple full-width rail and eyelet curtain sits comfortably within the original panelled interior*

8 *The master bedroom and bathroom have been created in the former garret workroom*

9 *Ground floor plan*

10 *First floor plan*

11 *Second floor plan*

12 *Third floor plan*

13 *Discreet lighting, electrics and radiators are carefully integrated into the existing fabric*

14 *Vitsoe classic contemporary shelving system leaves the original panelling undisturbed*

Photography by Mike Neale

New York|brownstone

New York, New York, USA
Aardvarchitecture

COLOUR

Colour was an important way to create a sense of depth: from the light- coloured living areas, all cut-out views are towards areas with darker finishes. Green was chosen as a natural complement to the slight red undertone of the bleached red oak.

LIGHT/VENTILATION

A series of interior windows distribute light evenly through the space. The reconfiguration of the sitting and dining rooms also reduced the length of the corridor, bringing additional light into the home. Restoring some of the window frames that had previously been painted shut helped to increase ventilation. Light was also controlled by adding perforated shades in the sitting/dining room, allowing garden views to be enjoyed while cutting back on heat entering the room.

FURNITURE

The furniture was chosen for its simplicity and scale. Most of the furniture is slightly smaller and lower than standard dimensions, to make the small spaces appear larger without sacrificing comfort. The palette was chosen to complement the architecture, with white felt and leather upholstery, with chromed or oak feet. In the main bedroom, the owners chose an heirloom Victorian four-poster bed and wardrobe.

ADVICE

It's important to think about the spaces that one needs to live in and the kind of space in which one is comfortable. It's important to balance period craftsmanship and detail with contemporary requirements, allowing both periods to enrich each other.

This building, from the turn of the 19th century, was originally designed as several apartments. But unlike the current arrangement, the apartments shared a single kitchen rather than each having their own. A dumb waiter was used to bring food from the basement kitchen to the apartments. "The apartments were too small for live-in help or full maid's quarters," says architect Lynnette Widder who, with architect Christian Volkmann, reworked the townhouse that now occupies part of this building. ■ Located in the West Village of New York City and surrounded by bluestones, the townhouse faces a schoolyard on one side and the gardens of neighbouring homes on the other side. Rented for several years, the home had suffered various upgrades over time. "The floor was badly pitted and the bathroom and kitchen had to be gutted," says Widder. Fortunately, a considerable amount of the original woodwork was intact, including the red oak bar in the kitchen and timber panelling in the dining and sitting rooms. ■ One of the main changes made to the two-bedroom home was to combine the sitting room with the dining room. "We also removed part of the wall in the corridor to allow for more generous light and garden views. Originally, the spaces gave the impression of being quite dark," says Widder. To screen the entry door from view, a cabinet with a fretted glass screen was integrated into the living areas. One of the challenges of the project was to respect the existing structure's strength while allowing for contemporary living. "Our design strategy was never to mimic the existing details, but instead juxtapose our additions by leaving a small gap between the old and new elements," she adds. ■ The original red oak was bleached to create a lighter feel and formed the basis for the palette of materials used. The new floor is bleached maple, while deep greens were selected for the kitchen cabinetry. The cut outs between rooms are framed by a flat-brushed stainless steel angle, akin to a contemporary picture frame. The cut outs, which run parallel to the home's long window wall, allow the spaces to feel interconnected. "We describe our interior work as 'spatial archaeology' through which we uncover the strongest qualities of a home, often obscured by earlier renovations," says Widder. ■

Opposite   *19th-century millwork in living room and kitchen is offset by the brushed stainless steel-framed vitrine*

2

3

4

The Ultimate Urban Makeover

167

2 *View from entry past the fretted glass screen*

3 *Living and dining rooms have been unified*

4 *Mahogany-stained woodwork in the kitchen provides foreground depth-of-field*

5 *Contrast of pale and vivid hues applies to material choices throughout apartment*

6 *View through privacy glass from shower to living room*

5

6

8

7 Kitchen pass-through frames the dining area
8 Reflective surfaces enlarge narrow bathroom

Photography by Paul Rivera, archphoto New York

1

1   Rear north-facing elevation with
    louvred balcony to upper bedroom;
    living room is below
2   Rear terrace to living area with living
    area alcove
3   View of rear terrace to living area
    showing powder room and laundry
    pods with old and new stairs beyond

2

3

One|of|three

Melbourne, Victoria, Australia
David Luck Architecture

CIRCULATION

For Luck, it was important to create an open-plan feel that was evident as soon as you enter the house. "We removed as many internal walls as possible. We wanted to open up the views, whether they were into the garden or simply into another room," says Luck.

LIGHT

A 2-metre-wide toughened-glass skylight acts as a transition space between the original house and the new wing. Pitched at 45 degrees, the roof is self-cleaning. Celestial windows over the new staircase also bring additional light into the interior spaces. One side of the second-storey addition is 80 percent glass. The bathrooms on the first floor feature frosted glass walls to shoulder height, allowing light to penetrate. A high slot window over the kitchen also brings light into the work areas.

FURNITURE

As the spaces are relatively small, the owners selected simple contemporary furniture, both for the original part of the house and the new wing. "It's a relatively flexible floor plan. My clients aren't fixed into using each space in a certain way. Furniture can be moved around," says Luck.

ADVICE

"It's better to have a few large spaces to relieve the home's narrow footprint. A few spaces at 5–6 metres wide are more suitable for contemporary living than a series of confined rooms," says Luck. "You should aim to have living areas the full width of the site, even if the site is only 6 metres wide," he adds. And while the row house is popular, finding a way to live in them today can be costly. "These sites are often costly to develop. The way we want to live today doesn't always translate to these long and narrow sites".

This double-storey row house is flanked by two identical homes. On a relatively narrow site, 6 metres wide by 30 metres deep, the 1890's brick home wasn't suitable in its original form for a couple with two small children. "Their brief was quite open. They wanted a more relaxed, informal style of living; something that reminded them of the warmer climate they left behind," says architect David Luck. ■ The original two rooms at the front of the house, on both the ground floor as well as the first floor, were retained. The ground-floor rooms were restored and are now used as the family's formal living area and as a separate dining area. To create a more fluid spatial arrangement, Luck removed the walls surrounding the fireplace in the living area. "The front rooms are reasonably large. But we wanted to create a strong connection to the new kitchen and informal living areas," says Luck. The two original rooms on the first floor of the house were also restored and are now used as the children's bedrooms. ■ To clearly delineate the new wing from the original part of the house, a 2-metre-wide glass roof was inserted between the dining area and the new wing. In contrast to the original home, the new wing is sleek and contemporary. The kitchen, for example, features a central island bench, clad in marble and polished timber floors. "The central bench is treated like a piece of furniture in the space. It's simple and streamlined," says Luck. Floor-to-ceiling glass doors to the small patio-style garden at the rear of the property were also included. A recess in one wall of the living area accommodates a lounge, adding width to the relatively narrow area. On the other side of the space, a low timber cabinet contains electronics, including the stereo system. ■ Upstairs, over the new living areas, are two bathrooms, (one used by the children, the other an ensuite) and the main bedroom, complete with balcony. A powder-coated aluminium-louvred balustrade on the balcony creates privacy from neighbouring homes, as do highlight windows in the main bedroom. A frosted-glass window was inserted adjacent to the floor in the main bedroom to provide additional light. "You get the morning light as well as privacy," says Luck. ■

4

5

6

8

9

4   Living room opens into kitchen; the dining room is beyond the new wall opening
5   Dining room in the original section with new wall openings framing kitchen and living room beyond
6   View into bedroom from balcony
7   Marble-clad kitchen island bench with living room beyond
8   Bedroom with powder-coated aluminium louvred screen beyond
9   New section of stair from original stair landing with glass roof and bathrooms beyond
10   Original stair with new wall openings framing dining room and kitchen beyond

Photography by Glenn Hester

7

10

Removing|the|locks

Melbourne, Victoria, Australia
JAM Architects (previously Jan|Manton Architecture)

CIRCULATION
The new wing was designed to draw people into the dining and living areas. Rather than extending the original shotgun corridor, the owners gravitate towards the light and increased volumes.

LIGHT/VENTILATION
A 10-metre-long skylight above the living and dining areas brings additional light into the new wing. A floor-to-ceiling window linking the original house with the new wing can be fully opened. This allows air to travel through the addition and the large aluminium and glass bi-fold doors to the terrace.

MATERIALS
The materials in this home are relatively restrained. Polished spotted gum timber floorboards continue from the front door to the rear terrace.

COLOUR
The timber veneer used for the joinery in the kitchen and the living area, provides the main colour. The chocolate grey colour of the timber is the main accent against white plaster walls.

ADVICE
"It's important to get the natural lighting right. Sometimes, this isn't obvious. In this case, we borrowed light from the skylight that runs the width of the new wing. We removed a plaster wall in the original dining room and inserted a sliding timber door. When it's left open the light spills out into the original rooms," says Manton.

This Victorian home, built in the late 1800s, was previously occupied by up to 10 university students. With so many people coming and going, it's not surprising that padlocks were put onto individual doors. "Every student protected their own turf," says architect Chris Manton. ■ The house had been rented for many years before it was purchased for a family. And while locks and cobwebs were removed from each room, fortunately many of the original features of the house were intact, including wide skirting boards, architraves and cornices, although the latter were badly cracked. ■ Two rooms on the ground floor were retained as the formal lounge and dining rooms. Four bedrooms on the first floor of the house were also retained, but it was a balancing act to keep the two rear bedrooms on the first floor. "Our brief was to create a new contemporary wing on the ground floor. When the additions on the ground floor had been removed, the level above was precariously perched above a demolition site." Although the original stables at the rear of the property were retained, they were unfortunately not suitable for conversion into a garage. "We simply removed the roof and kept the heritage-listed brick walls. This space is now part of the garden," says Manton. As the land slopes 3 metres from the street, a basement level was incorporated and is now used as a glass blowing studio. ■ Once past the restored timber staircase, the house opens into a large open-plan living area. The kitchen and living area occupy the entire width of the site, while the dining area is adjacent to a new laundry and leads directly onto a terrace. A skylight was inserted along the edge of the new living areas to create additional light. A new floor-to-ceiling window was also added to the side of the house, where the original house finishes and the new wing begins (the new wing extends to the side boundary, unlike the original house, which is set back 1.2 metres from the boundary). ■ The kitchen features a simple palette of materials including stone bench tops, timber-veneer cupboards and frosted-glass overhead cupboards. And while the lines are simple, there is subtle decoration in the form of timber louvres in the floor to allow for heating and cooling. Timber louvres also appear on one side of the kitchen's central island bench, concealing the heating unit behind. ■ The new wing, constructed in rendered brick, steel, glass and aluminium, is considerably lighter in feel than the original home. The circulation in this area also differs, with the path to the rear terrace circling the

(continued)

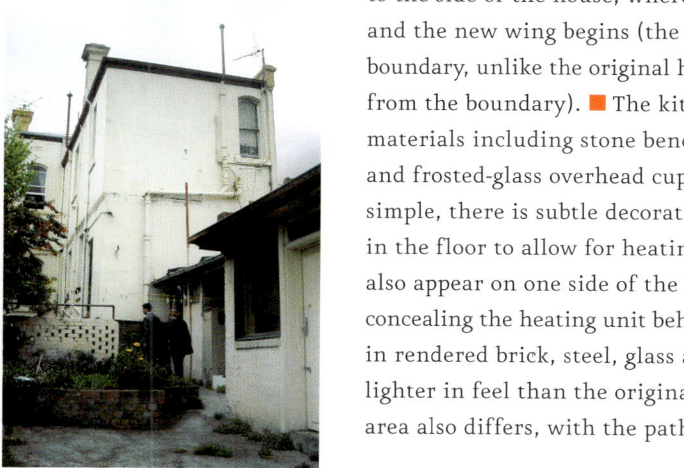

2   3

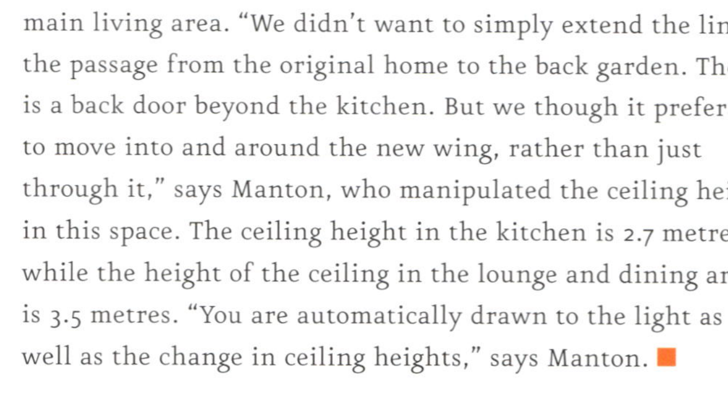

4

5

6

main living area. "We didn't want to simply extend the line of the passage from the original home to the back garden. There is a back door beyond the kitchen. But we though it preferable to move into and around the new wing, rather than just through it," says Manton, who manipulated the ceiling heights in this space. The ceiling height in the kitchen is 2.7 metres, while the height of the ceiling in the lounge and dining areas is 3.5 metres. "You are automatically drawn to the light as well as the change in ceiling heights," says Manton. ■

7

4   Rear yard during demolition
5   Rear bedroom wing propped during demolition
6   Demolition of existing interior
7   Completed rear elevation and terrace
8   Completed rear elevation

The Ultimate Urban Makeover

Removing the locks

11

12

13

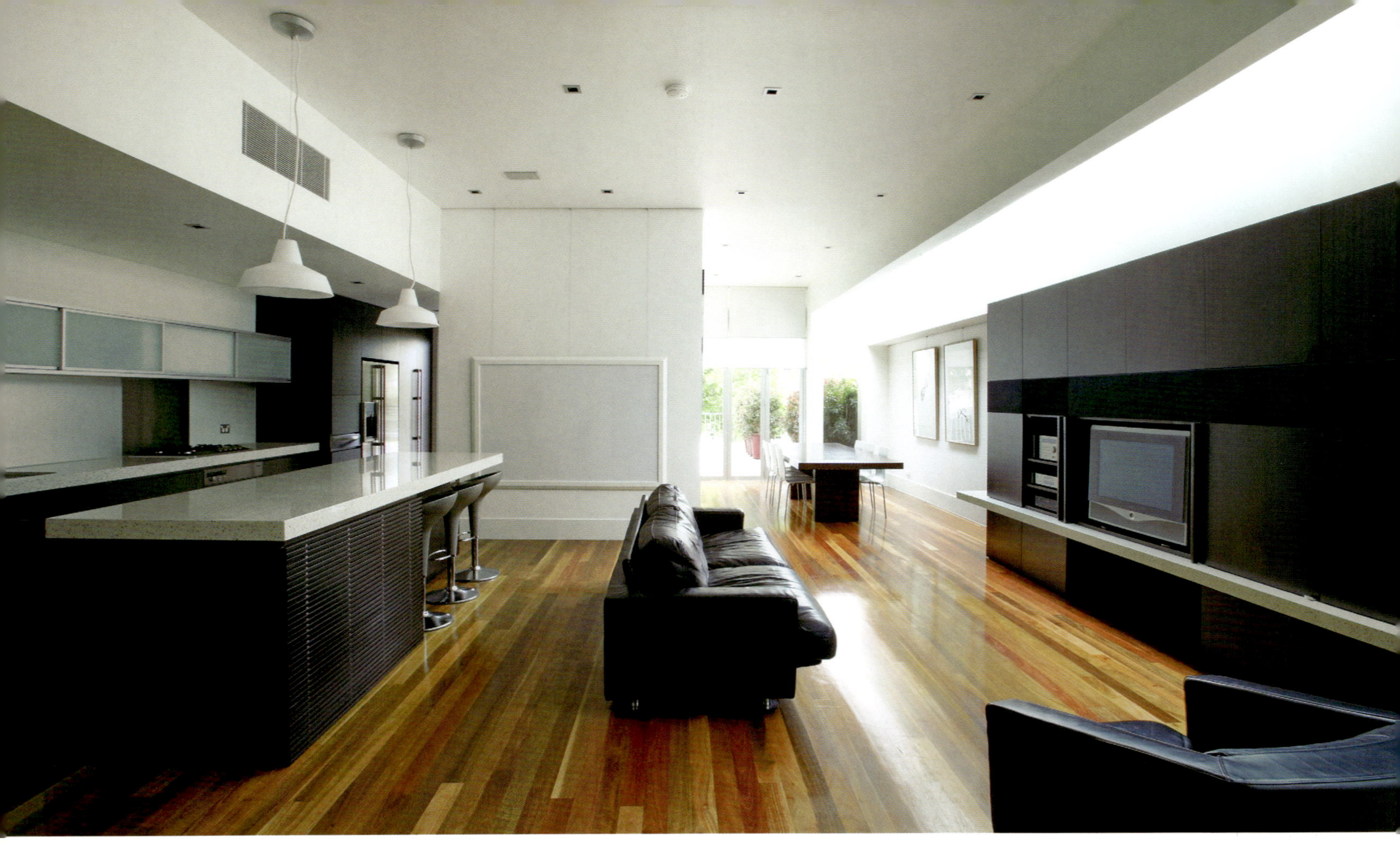

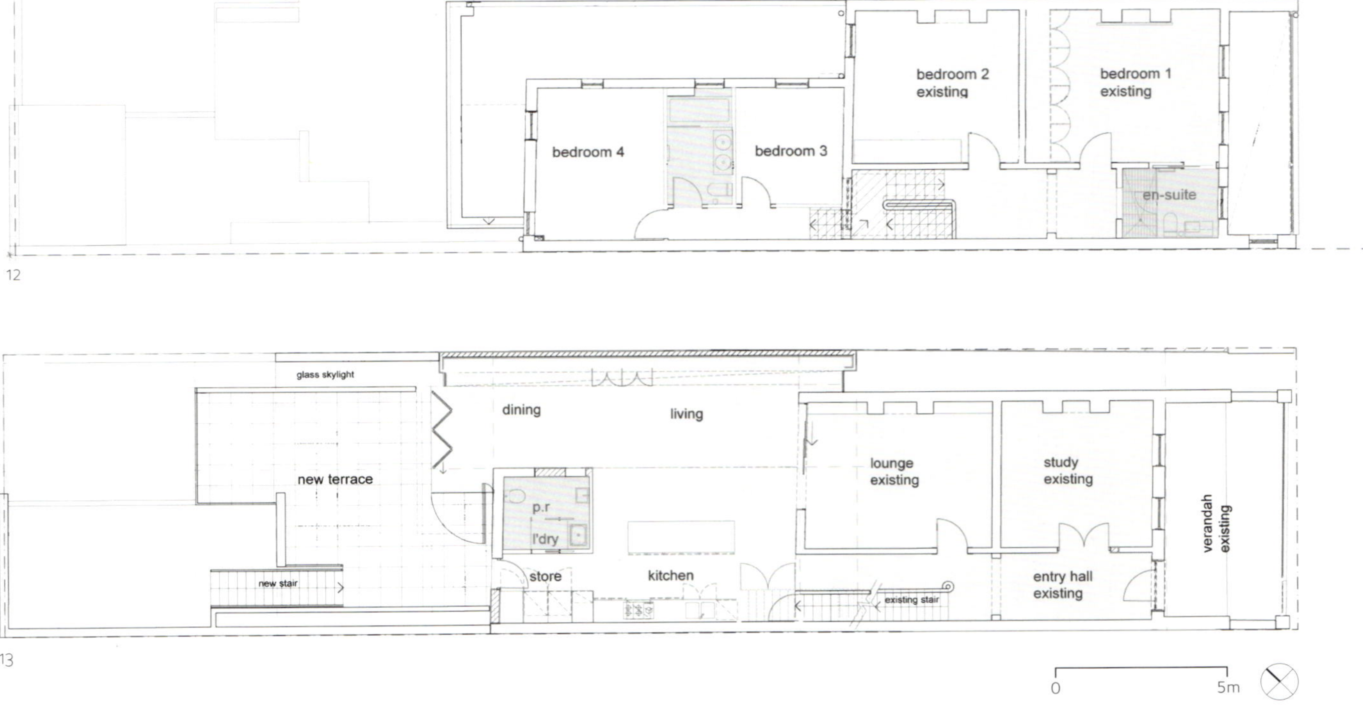

11 *Open-plan living/kitchen and dining area*

12 *First floor plan*

13 *Ground floor plan*

Opposite *View through living area to rear terrace*

15

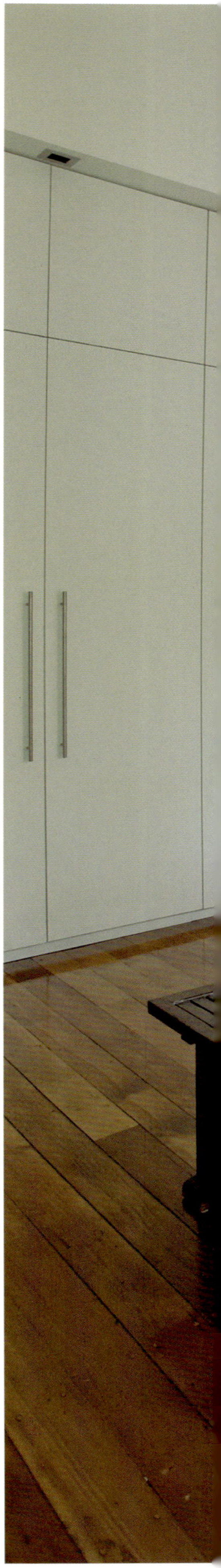

16

15 Bathroom
16 Master bedroom

Photography by Sharyn Cairnes (1,7–11, 14–16)
Jan Manton Architecture (3)
James Grant (2,4–6)

The Ultimate Urban Makeover

1   *The cross-shaped window on the east side welcomes in the morning light*

2   *Night view; the garden area is now larger than it was, despite the floor area increasing significantly*

3   *House before renovation*

Restrained|Victorian

Albert Park, Victoria, Australia
Nicholas Gioia Associates

Energy efficiency
Windows were double glazed, and are externally shaded to prevent excessive heat gain; walls and ceilings are insulated to a greater degree than required by regulations.

Light/Ventilation
Only natural lighting is used inside during daylight hours. Opening doors and windows were placed to ensure maximum cross ventilation.

Materials
Because of the budget involved, a commitment was made to use basic, economical materials and finishes. Readily available, easily maintained, off-the-shelf components and commonplace construction techniques were used. Expensive finishes and complex detailing were deliberately minimised. The base structure is timber-framed, the walls are brick veneer and the roof is corrugated zincalume on a timber frame. Interior finishes are also low cost and low maintenance and include plasterboard, polished floorboards and plastic laminates. Luxury materials such as marble are restricted to the kitchen and one bathroom.

Advice
Expensive materials, finishes and construction techniques don't necessarily produce a superior house. The simplicity of low-maintenance, sustainable materials can be a powerful architectural statement in itself.

This charming house is located in Albert Park, a genteel inner suburb of Melbourne developed in the latter part of the 19th century and in which Victorian houses predominate. The street is wide but the site felt hemmed in. ■ "The client wanted to solve the problems typical of Victorian homes," says architect Nicholas Gioia. "It was important to overcome the lack of outlook and the claustrophobic and gloomy interiors." ■ The addition has been designed to take full advantage of the site by creating as much interior space as possible, allowing views onto landscaped areas and letting in controllable sunlight. It allows the clients to experience the exhilaration of space, through extensive, but protected glazing and discreet skylights that allow light to pour through the entire house. ■ A critical requirement was to not impose upon the neighbouring houses. The resulting addition is compact and 'contained', and has not altered the neighbours' amenity, allowing them as much daylight as they received with the existing house. ■ The reorganisation of spaces and functions externally and internally is simple: the client wanted the bedrooms to face the street and the living areas to face a private outdoor living area. The result is that the bedrooms are at the front, the bathroom and laundry are in the middle and the kitchen, dining and living rooms are at the rear where they face a secluded courtyard that can accommodate a car if required. The courtyard also has two tiny sheds for bicycles, tools and firewood. The living areas and bathroom also face a second courtyard in the middle of the house. ■ A tight budget led to the choice of simple, over-the-counter building materials and finishes. The external cladding materials selected, brick and corrugated zincalume, are simply a reflection of the materials that predominate in the area. ■ The project proposes a prototype for the rejuvenation or renewal of a common inner-suburban housing type: the attached house. It shows that even if such a building is constricted by neighbours, it can still feel spacious, admit abundant controllable sunlight, have views in many directions and have an adaptable ambience. ■

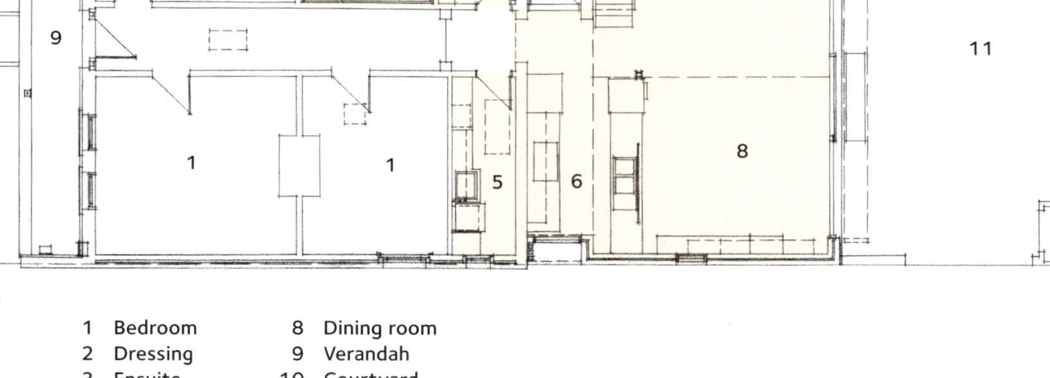

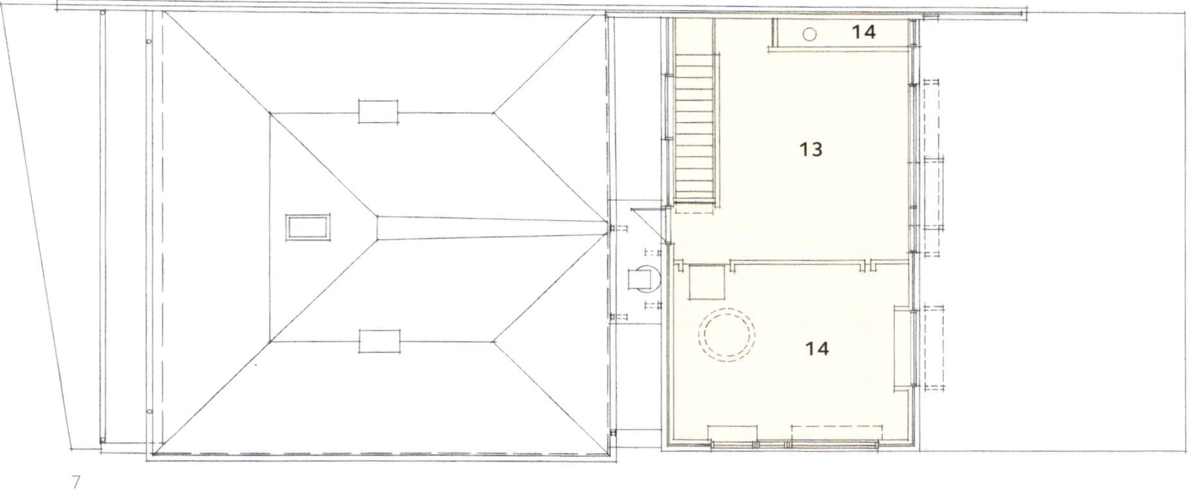

1	Bedroom	8	Dining room
2	Dressing	9	Verandah
3	Ensuite	10	Courtyard
4	Bathroom	11	Garden
5	Laundry	12	Store
6	Kitchen	13	Mezzanine
7	Living room	14	Void

Opposite *The double-height space of the dining area provides relief from the hemmed-in feeling of the original house*

5 *The mezzanine with the double-height space beyond*

6 *View of the mezzanine hovering over the living room*

7 *Mezzanine floor plan*

8 *Ground floor plan*

9

10

11

9 Dramatic, ever-changing sunlight patterns made by the differently shaped windows and skylights

10 The interior has direct views over the garden and framed views of the sky

11 Bathroom

12 North side windows are shaded by sunscreens that still allow entry of winter sunlight

13 Night lighting can be adjusted to provide an ambience that ranges from cocooning to exhilarating

Photography by Trevor Mein (1,4–6,9,11–13)
John Gollings (2,10)
Nicholas Gioia (3)

Room|for a|family

Sydney, New South Wales, Australia
Cullen Feng Architects

CIRCULATION
The narrow passage leading from the front door was widened to create a sense of arrival. Space from the original front room was commandeered. "It's an extremely narrow terrace. But that doesn't mean you should feel cramped," says Feng. The original staircase was relocated between the guest bathroom and the new kitchen. A freestanding stainless steel island bench, featuring an integrated stainless steel sink, facilitates circulation in the kitchen.

FURNITURE
As space was limited, built-in furniture was incorporated into the design. An entertainment unit, for example, was built into the living space. Suspended from the wall, the unit appears to float in space. "You can see the entire floor space. And in this case, every centimetre counts," says Feng. Likewise, rather than cluttering the rear garden with furniture, a simple timber garden bench sits along one wall, giving children room to play.

DETAIL
In contrast to the ornate iron lacework framing the original façade, the rear elevation is simple and contemporary. For the balustrades enclosing the deck from the main bedroom, Feng used perforated steel plates. "It was important to keep the heritage façade intact. But we wanted to created a contemporary edge to the rear," says Feng, who also included a retractable steel awning outside the living area. "When it's extended, it doubles the length of the living space. The garden becomes another room," she says.

COLOUR
The walls in this home, both in the original and new sections, are white. Colour appears in the richness of the karri timber floors.

ADVICE
"It's important to relate the living spaces to the outside wherever possible. If the garden is at the rear, the kitchen and living areas should follow," says Feng. And in a small terrace such as this one, Feng suggests avoiding clutter. "You have to be extremely discerning about what you want and what you actually need."

This inner-city terrace was bought by a couple who were living overseas at the time. When they returned with one child and another on the way, they realised that their terrace wasn't suitable for a family. It wasn't only the number of rooms that were inadequate, the condition of the building was also a problem. "It was fairly basic. It was structurally sound, but there were a series of lean-tos, including an external toilet," says architect Michelle Feng. ■ One of the biggest problems with the terrace was its width, a mere 3.6 metres. To compensate for this, the ceiling heights in the new kitchen and living areas were accentuated. "We were fortunate to have a 3-metre slope across the land. After excavating at the rear, there was also enough room to include a garage," says Feng. ■ Two formal front rooms in the original Victorian home were completely reworked. One room was converted into a study and guest bathroom. Part of this room was also used to extend the corridor, initially quite narrow. The other room was incorporated into the new kitchen. The upstairs rooms were also redesigned, with a main bedroom, robe and ensuite added to the rear of the building. ■ Some of the original features, such as skirting boards, were removed from the house. "We had to remove some of the Victorian features to make way for the new rooms," says Feng. "There was no point trying to reinsert these into a new bathroom," she adds. The original timber staircase was also sacrificed in the renovation, as the risers were far too steep, for adults as well as children. "The stairs also cut up the spaces," says Feng, who inserted a new timber staircase behind the kitchen joinery. ■

Opposite *Restored Victorian façade*

2 View of original house from rear

3 Existing ramshackle ground-floor addition

4 Original courtyard seen from above (level raised to accommodate double garage)

5 New rear courtyard with custom planters and mirror stainless water feature

Opposite New two-storey rear façade

2

3

4

5

8
9
10

11

8 Original front rooms of house
9 Original stair
10 New stair viewed from first level
11 New living area with courtyard beyond
12 First floor plan
13 Ground floor plan
14 Basement floor plan

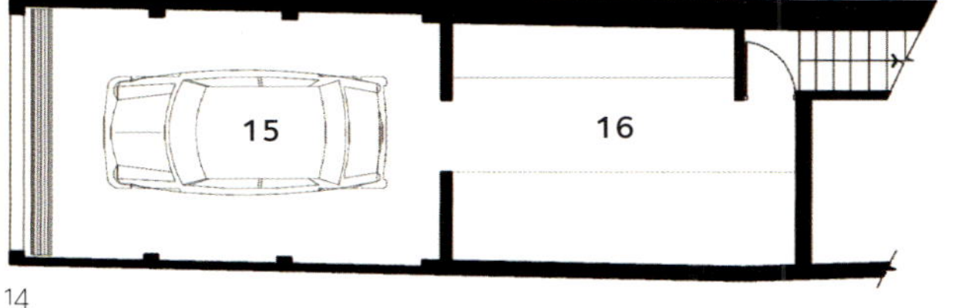

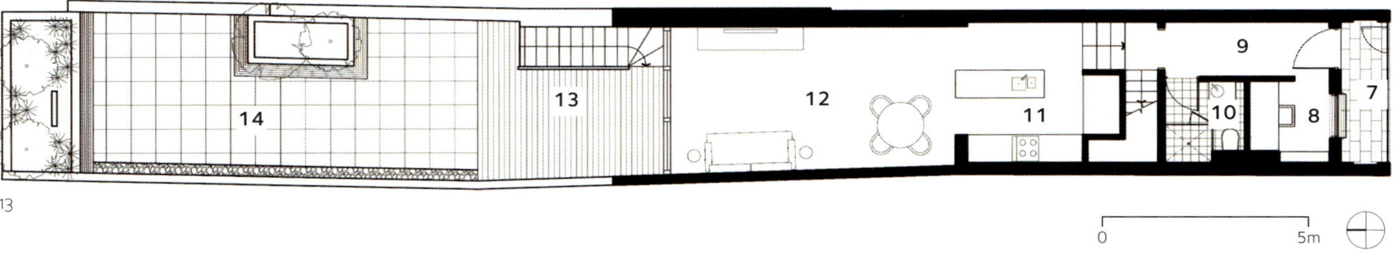

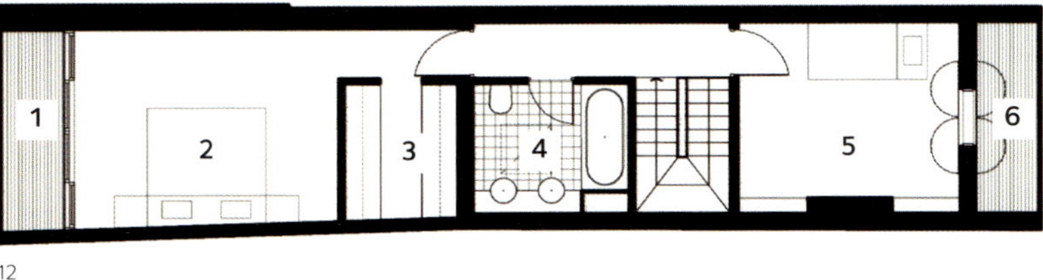

1 Balcony
2 Main bedroom
3 Robe
4 Bath
5 Bedroom
6 Balcony
7 Entry porch
8 Study
9 Hallway
10 Guest bath
11 Kitchen
12 Living/dining
13 Terrace
14 Terrace
15 Garage
16 Store

16

17

15   New kitchen with stainless steel island bench
16   New main bedroom with balcony overlooking rear courtyard
17   New main bathroom

Photography by Murray Fredericks

1

Spanish|with a|secret

Los Angeles, California, USA

Abramson Teiger Architects

COLOUR

Natural materials were used to create the exterior colour scheme. Teak-stained vertical cedar siding, weathered galvalume metal siding, and a light and dark integrated colour stucco establish a warm palette.

LIGHT

The open floor plan allows visual continuity between the different spaces. A large 5- x 5-foot skylight over the bed in the master bedroom allows views of the night sky.

FURNITURE

Architect Douglas Teiger designed several of the pieces himself, including the dining table. The fabrics and materials of the furniture are kept to neutral tones to complement the natural materials of the house. A small table designed for the younger children is just outside the kitchen.

ADVICE

Making small spaces feel larger is an architect's magic. Douglas Teiger transformed the traditional living room into an art gallery/entry, making this small house feel larger. Use a technique such as painting a single wall of a room with an accent of a darker colour to expand the depth of the room.

This 1300-square-foot home, built in the 1920s, was bursting at the seams. With a growing family and the parents' desire for additional space and privacy, the previously typical single-storey Spanish-style house is now a two-storey 2500-square-foot contemporary home with all the conveniences a young family requires, and lots of fun spaces for the kids. ■ The idea of a traditional living room was discarded in favour of a gallery/foyer where architect Douglas Teiger can display his own paintings and sculpture as well as work by other artists. Walking into this space off the street is truly like walking into an art gallery – the only difference being a view to the dining room through the archway that is flanked on either side by carved wood pillars from India. ■ The master bedroom and children's room are located on the new second floor. The high ceiling in the children's room has been designed to accommodate a future sleeping loft, making the current room into a play/work room with desks and other requirements for older children. A narrow closet space in the upstairs hallway conceals a ladder leading to the children's secret hideaway. "This room is like a treehouse inside the house," says Teiger. "The floor is covered in a very large beanbag so the boys can jump off the ladder on their way down." ■ Teiger decided early on that the garage, a separate freestanding structure in the back garden, would be an ideal full-sized playhouse for his active boys. The playhouse is in full view of the kitchen and the large sliding doors to the garden are left open so the children and their friends have constant free access to the main house, the playhouse and the garden. The property is completely fenced off from the street for privacy and safety. ■ The playhouse floor is covered in sponge letter tile that serves two purposes – rough play without injury and a way of learning the alphabet and the colours as well. Chairs and tables in appropriate size for young children are provided along with ample storage and lots of interesting toys. In the garden outside the kids' house is a small patio where the family can gather for lunch in the pleasant Californian climate. ■

2

1   *Front walkway is a sculptural series of concrete cubes cascading towards the sidewalk*

2   *Front before renovation; the original porte-cochère remains intact to maintain setbacks*

3

4

1 Entry
2 Living room
3 Dining room
4 Kitchen
5 Breakfast area
6 Master bathroom
7 Master bedroom
8 Closet
9 Hall
10 Bathroom
11 Linen closet
12 Bedroom 2

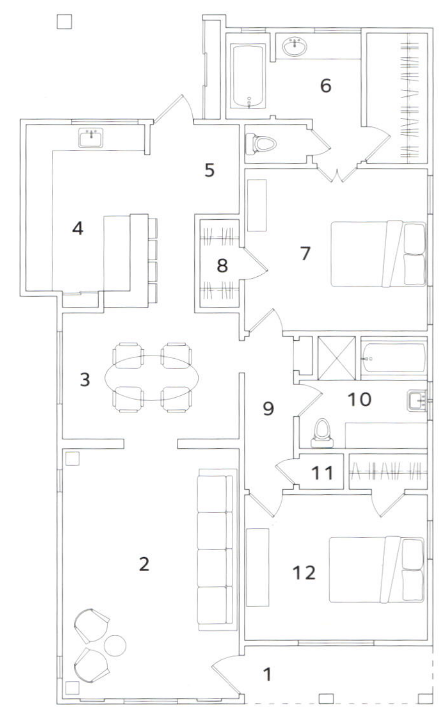

5

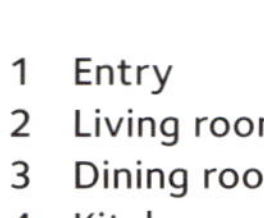

6

The Ultimate Urban Makeover

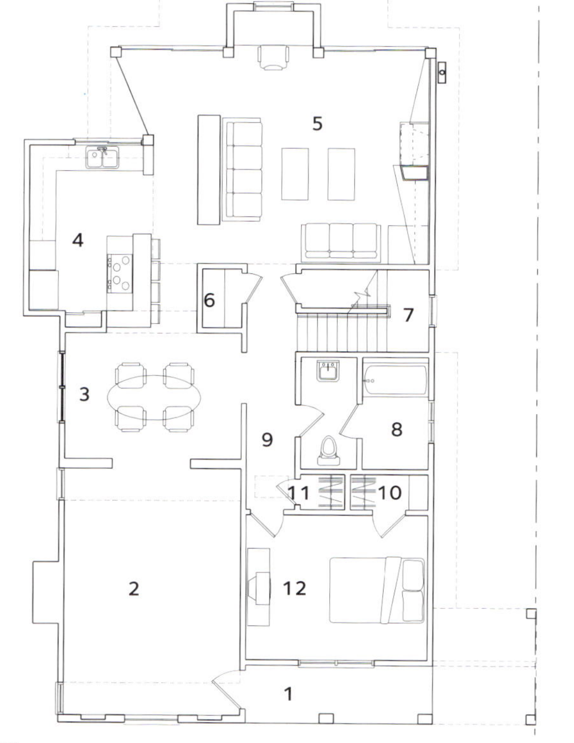

3 The master bedroom has a ceiling that soars to 17 feet with a dramatic 6-foot-square
   skylight and an accent wall to add depth to a narrow room
4 The powder room uses the same floor tile as an accent wall behind the sink
5 Floor plan before
6 15-foot ceilings make the narrow master bathroom feel much larger
7 Birch veneer bi-fold doors hide the laundry, linen closets and entry to the secret room
8 Custom ladder provides access to the secret room
9 A skylight floods the small hideaway, creating a tree house inside the house
10 Ground floor plan after
11 First floor plan after

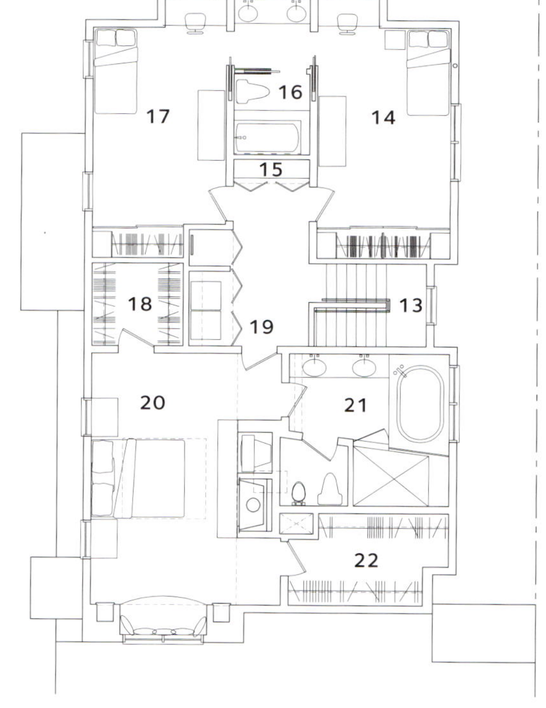

1   Entry
2   Art gallery
3   Dining room
4   Kitchen
5   Family room
6   Closet
7   Stair
8   Bathroom
9   Hall
10 Closet
11 Closet
12 Guest bedroom
13 Stair landing
14 Bedroom 2
15 Linen closet
16 Bathroom
17 Bedroom 1
18 His closet
19 Hall
20 Master bedroom
21 Master bathroom
22 Her closet

12

13

14

12   Kitchen
13   A small-scale table is just right for the
     young boys in the family
14   View from art gallery through dining
     room towards kitchen and garden
15   The glass wall makes the dining room
     feel bigger while allowing light into the
     hallway beyond.
16   The sculptural wood trellis plays off the
     roof angles of the main house to link
     the pool and house as a single
     composition

Photography by John Ellis (1,3,4,12,14,15)
          Douglas Teiger (2,7–9,13)
          John Linden (16)

15

16

Steeped|in|history

Clerkenwell, London, UK
Derek Wylie Architects

COLOUR

The interior features the natural tones and colour of the materials, whether oak, limestone (bathrooms), glass or metal. Colour is introduced through furniture that can be changed at any time.

LIGHT/VENTILATION

Glass-brick walls and ceiling in the basement allow additional light to enter. Glass is also used in combination with timber in the mezzanine floor in the study. Even the staircases have been designed with light in mind, the main staircase featuring a woven mesh steel balustrade. To improve the home's ventilation, trickle vents were installed in the frames of the new glass doors and windows at ground level.

FURNITURE

Furniture was selected to provide colour within the neutral interior. The furniture was also selected to enable layout changes. The dining table, for example, was specifically made for easy relocation into either the courtyard or living area. A few fixed pieces of built-in furniture were designed. A linear wall storage unit in the den is made of aluminium, laminate and mesh. The wardrobes in the bedrooms are made of canvas.

ADVICE

The most successful renovations always seem to be those that have retained the essential character of the original house. This includes not only decorative features such as fireplaces and cornices, but also the 'big' architecture of the house such as form, structure, layout, construction and the materials, which contribute far more to the personality of any building.

1   *Street lobby provides entrance to house, office and apartment*
2   *Corner sliding doors open living areas into courtyard*
3   *Stepped entrance ramp*

This townhouse was once a centre for breweries, distilleries and the printing industry. These industries have moved to other parts of the city, with craft workshops now proliferating in the area. Many former industrial buildings, like this one, have recently been converted into loft dwellings. ■ Architect Derek Wylie found the site in a virtually derelict state. "It comprised a four-storey townhouse and silversmith workshop. But apart from the small courtyard separating the two, it felt relatively enclosed. Natural light and views were limited," says Wylie, who converted the silversmith workshop into a townhouse for a couple with two children. ■ While the structure of the workshop was relatively intact, the interior had been stripped out and painted black (having previously been used as a rave venue). The ground-floor shop of approximately 250 square metres was transformed into an office, and the former basement storage areas became the large bathroom/sauna and utility areas. As the ground floor of the silversmiths had originally been open plan, it was suitable for the new living areas in the townhouse. Two rooms upstairs, once studios, are now bedrooms. ■ "My clients were keen that the house should be robust and capable of withstanding the attentions of land-locked children who enjoyed sports," says Wylie. The lack of windows was addressed by creating new roof light areas at the natural junction between the four-storey townhouse and the former workshop. A glass brick floor/ceiling over the basement also brings in additional light. An existing toilet block, located on the corner of the building, was removed to create a small courtyard. ■ The design approach was to insert the new structures and construction into the surviving shell, to provide dramatic contrasts between old and new. The existing brick walls were exposed by shot blasting the bricks. Surviving joints, structural holes and original timber beams were also left in place. ■ The glazed infill extension between the original townhouse and silversmith workshop now forms an entrance hall with a mezzanine study area above. Alternating oak and glass planks in the mezzanine floor increase light in the hall below. The kitchen is constructed from two materials: the work surfaces are formed from terrazzo concrete using a specially designed mould; the kitchen structure, which was designed as a continuous freestanding wall, is constructed from plywood formed on metal studs and clad in aluminium. ■ New staircases, featuring oak steps and steel

(continued)

4

4 Entrance hall and mezzanine roof light
5 Full-length roof light lets daylight into kitchen
6 Night view showing new roof lights and balcony perched over courtyard
7 Top to bottom: first floor plan, ground floor plan, basement floor plan
8 Mast staircase at rear suggests physical separation of functions

5

The Ultimate Urban Makeover

balustrades, suggest physical separation between different functions in the living area, without spoiling the continuity of the space. "The materials I've used in the renovation – timber, stone, concrete and glass – reflect the materials found in the original shell. There's a sense of honesty and solidity from both the past and present," says Wylie. ■

1 Street lobby
2 House entrance
3 Stepped ramp
4 Office
5 Kitchen
6 Dining
7 TV den
8 Living
9 Courtyard
10 Pool
11 Bedroom
12 Balcony
13 Void
14 Bathroom
15 Mezzanine
16 Sauna room
17 Utility
18 Adjoining roof
19 Apartment entrance
20 Adjoining properties
21 First-floor apartment

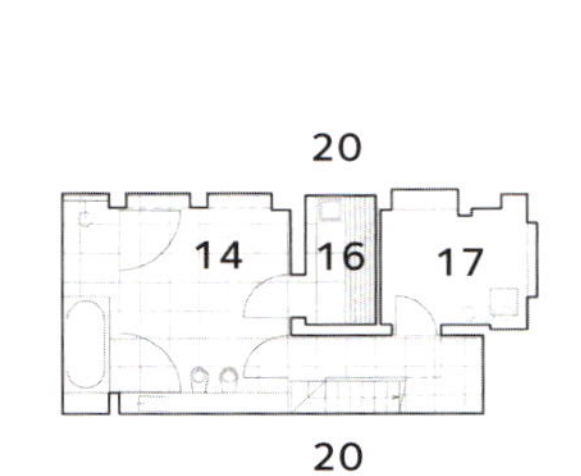

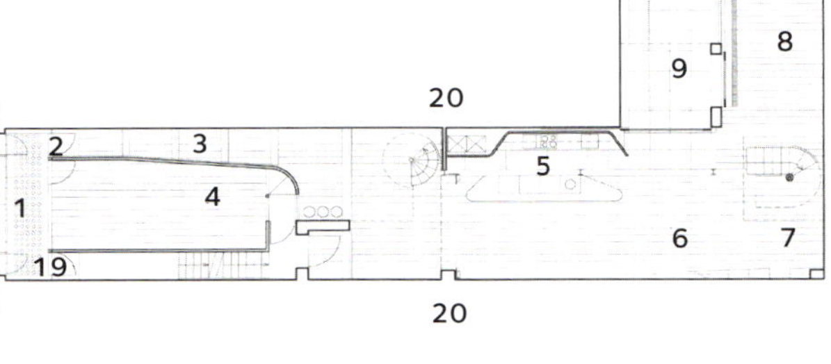

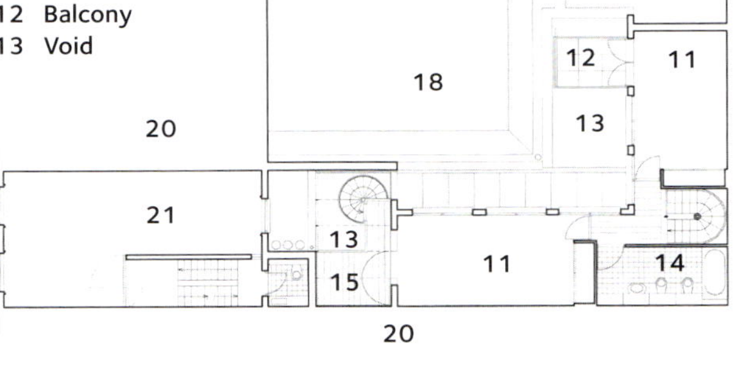

9

9   *Movable furniture in living areas allows flexible arrangements*

10 *Beehive storage wall at first-floor bathroom*

11 *Existing and new construction elements merge and contrast in master bedroom/mezzanine area*

12 *Space and light at basement wet room*

13 *Steel and oak flitch construction reduces weight of new architectural elements*

14 *Steel fabric and glass planks maximise daylight into ground floor areas*

15 *Glass bricks at street lobby floor above wet room*

Photography by Nick Kane

10

11

12

13

14

15

1

2

3

4

1 *View of terrace with bluestone lane to north*
2 *Side gates can be opened, allowing access to lane*
3 *Bluestone lanes are part of urban texture of inner-city Melbourne*
4 *Deep highlight glazing to north captures autumn and winter sun*

Textured|modernism

Parkville, Victoria, Australia
BURO Architects – Interiors by Hecker Phelan Guthrie

COLOUR
The walls and ceiling are white. The only colour used in the renovation is a bright lobster-red carpet in the living and study areas. There is also an acid-green door leading to the ensuite bathroom. The robinia in the rear courtyard displays an impressive show of lime-coloured leaves during the summer months. The green leaves are reflected on the white walls in the bedroom.

MATERIALS
The palette of materials used in the renovation was kept simple. The timber floorboards are lacquered in black. The joinery in the kitchen is also dark, featuring stained American oak, while the benches and splashbacks are lighter, made of marble. In contrast to the dark timber used in the kitchen, the joinery in the bedroom is MDF, painted a gloss white.

LIGHT/VENTILATION
Floor-to-ceiling glass doors were inserted into the kitchen and dining area. Highlight windows in the bedroom also draw in the sunlight.

Operable highlight windows in the bedroom allow hot air to escape in the warmer months. To allow the kitchen and dining area to cool down, large glass doors to the side courtyard can be left open. Slatted timber blinds in all the rooms also reduce the amount of heat entering the home.

FURNITURE
The owners' contemporary furniture collection includes the Hans Wegner chairs in the dining area, chairs by Verner Panton and chairs from some of the best contemporary designers. There are also African stools dotted around the house. Furniture passes through the house to their respective offices, then back again, depending on space.

ADVICE
Don't rush into the design. If you can, live in the house for a year to experience the four seasons. You can then assess the light conditions and design accordingly.

It's difficult to believe this Victorian cottage, circa 1895, once accommodated a family with five daughters. "The previous family bought the house in 1931 and lived here for more than 60 years," says architect Stephen Javens, who lives in the house with his partner, interior designer Kerry Phelan. While the house appeared relatively intact, there were an endless number of cupboards that had been removed. "There were at least 20 layers of wallpaper," adds Javens. ■ The house, which is located on the city fringe, occupies a long and narrow site, about 4 metres wide and 33 metres deep. However, while the site is narrow, it adjoins a laneway. "The laneway and the resulting access to light attracted us to the house in the first instance," says Javens. ■ Javens and Phelan retained the original front living room, together with a bedroom that led from the main corridor. But instead of creating two separate rooms, the wall between the two was removed. In the process, the original bedroom was transformed into a study. This open-plan area leads directly to a new kitchen and dining area. The only division between the old and new is a slight change in level, via a single step. Unlike the original front part of the house that retains Victorian detailing such as cornices, architraves and fireplace, the new wing is pared back. "The step acts as a threshold between the old and new. But we were keen to create the same volume in the kitchen and dining area," says Javens. ■ To capitalise on the laneway, large glass doors now lead to a side courtyard garden. Gates incorporated into the side fence can be opened to the laneway, to accommodate larger gatherings. ■ The kitchen and dining area lead to the main bedroom at the rear of the house. This room also opens to a small courtyard. "It's quite a simple arrangement. There are no doors, except for the bathroom. The design is more about a sequence of spaces and walking from a bright space (living areas) into a darker and more moody one," says Javens. The design also provides a backdrop for the couple's art and collection of artefacts, from Asia and the Middle East. As Javens says, "We're both interested in textured modernism. We were inspired by post-war Scandinavian designers such as Aalto and Jacobsen." ■

5

6

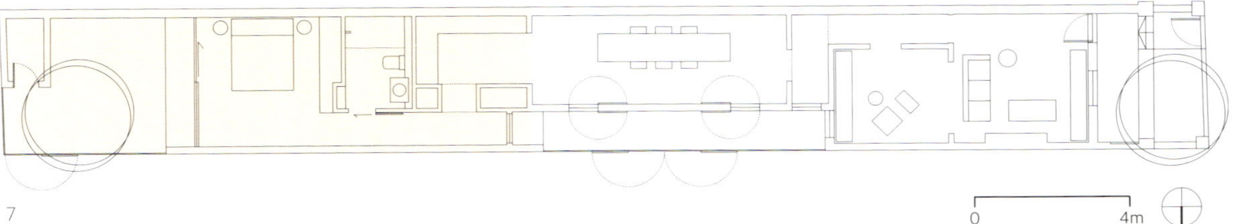

7

8
9

5 *View of dining room and kitchen with all-natural timbers and stone*
6 *View of bedroom; bathroom is behind acid-green door*
7 *Floor plan*
8 *Plants are used to provide shade and soften inner-city textures*
9 *View from existing house into north light court*
10 *View of long gallery towards courtyard garden*
11 *Artworks and artefacts grouped together into subtle arrangements*

Photography by Stephen Javens (1–4,8,9)
Earl Carter (5,6,10,11)

10

11

A|worker's|cottage

South Melbourne, Victoria, Australia
Kister Architects

LIGHT

One of the most important elements of terrace renovation is attracting sufficient light. The side courtyard acted as a lightwell in this renovation. New skylights above the original staircase add light to the home's central core. "I used predominantly light colours, such as white, on the walls," says Kister.

PRIVACY

As terrace homes are often in the shadow of their neighbours, creating privacy is important. Kister used a low, angular-shaped window in the new meals area to take advantage of the courtyard garden view. In the kitchen, a highlight angular window now draws in the sky rather than a neighbouring window.

MATERIALS

The rear façade features black glazed bricks and stained black timber doors. "I wanted to create a sense of solidity in the new work, similar to the solid masonry walls used in the terrace," says Kister. The floorboards in the new section are stained black and are laid horizontally, distinguishing them from the floorboards in the original part of the house. The wide skirting boards in the living room were carried through to the new wing. "It's important to get the balance right," says Kister.

ADVICE

Buy a terrace for its charm and because you love it. But you should realise that the affection comes with a price. There's often a problem with light. And in many cases, the spaces can be tight.

Opposite   *View of new rear cranked wall to extension*

Built in the 1870s, this Victorian terrace originally consisted of two rooms downstairs and two identically sized rooms upstairs. A two-storey lean-to, comprising a kitchen and upstairs bathroom, had been added during the 1950s. While the living room at the front of the house and the main bedroom upstairs were retained, the remainder was completely redesigned. "It didn't work for my clients. They needed extra space as well as extra light," says architect Ilana Kister. ■ The dining area adjacent to the formal living area was remodelled and became the new kitchen. A guest bathroom was also added in this space. "Guests shouldn't have to go up and down the stairs to reach a bathroom," says Kister. The new kitchen features angular bench tops and windows to a small courtyard on one side of the terrace. The 1950's lean-to was demolished and in its place a new meals area was created, complete with large timber and glass doors that open onto a deck. ■ The rear façade and the new interior appear to have been skewed. While the angular lines create interest, they were deliberately orchestrated. "There are strict guidelines in the area relating to setbacks. The design of the extension is really a response to these controls," says Kister. The 3-metre-high doors open onto a timber deck used for alfresco dining. "I wanted to increase the size of the meals area and take the floor space as far as possible," says Kister, who was conscious of the constraints the terrace posed. "It's only 3.6 metres wide. It was also about creating vertical space." High ceilings were also included in the renovation. ■ The existing second bedroom on the first level was considered too small for a bedroom and was converted into a bathroom. There was sufficient space above the new wing to create another bedroom. The brief included a third bedroom/study, which is tucked away on the third level of the house and is accessed by its own staircase. ■ While the renovation only added 50 square metres to the original floor plate, it has turned a cottage into a family home. ■

2   Interior view of the now-demolished original kitchen/meals area
3   Original rear façade
4   First floor plan before
5   Ground floor plan before
6   Roof plan after
7   First floor plan after
8   Ground floor plan after
9   Detail of rear façade

1   Living
2   Dining
3   Kitchen
4   Bedroom 1
5   Bedroom 2
6   Bathroom

The Ultimate Urban Makeover

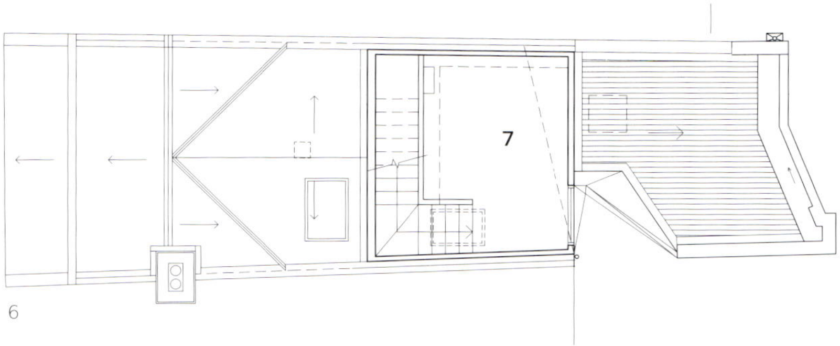

6

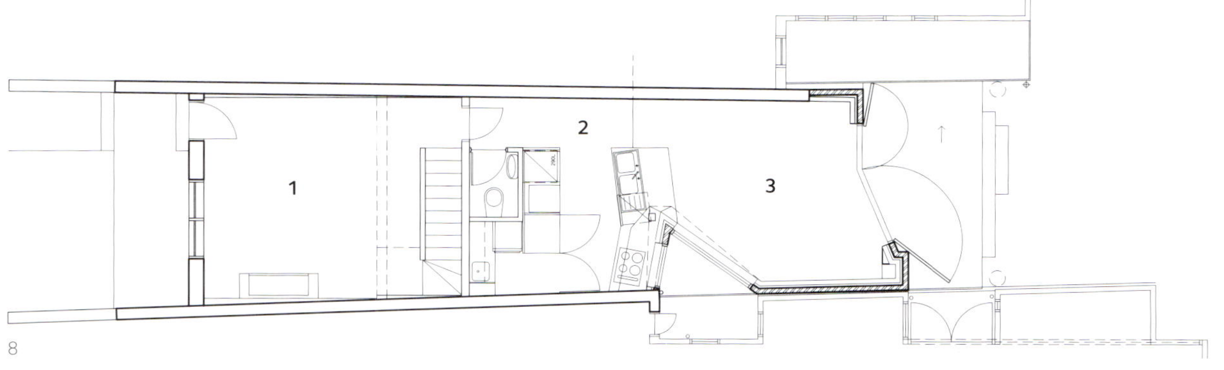

7

1 Living
2 Kitchen/powder room
3 Dining
4 Bedroom 1
5 Bathroom
6 Bedroom 2
7 Study/bedroom 3

8

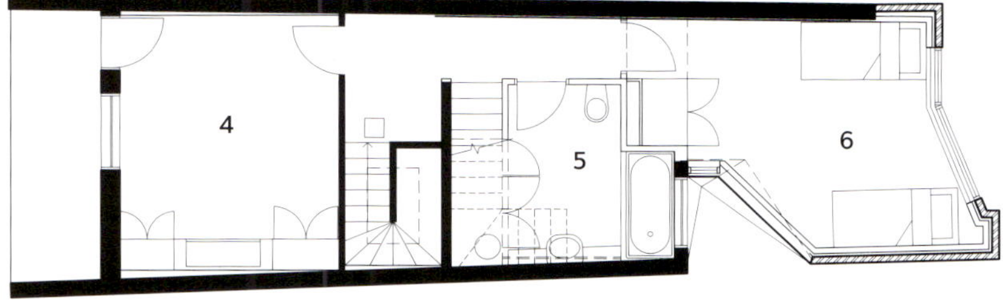

9

10   *New bedroom on upper level*
11   *New meals area*

Photography by Andrew Ashton

10

Acknowledgments

I would like to thank all the featured architects and owners featured. Their dedication in commissioning and designing these wonderful renovations is clearly expressed in the pages of this book. Thanks must also go to the many photographers who contributed. Their images allow these fabulous houses to be enjoyed by all of us.

I would also like to thank my partner Naomi for her support and literary criticism.